Roberta

D1197299

PUT GOD ON MAIN STREET

PUT GOD
ON MAIN STREET

an autobiography

BY

REX HUMBARD

As Told To Joyce Parks

Published under the auspices of
The Cathedral of Tomorrow, Inc., 1970

To Maude Aimee. . .
My beloved wife. . .
Mother of our four
children. . .
Faithful co-worker for
twenty-eight years in the
work of the Lord.

FOREWORD

One day when I was a boy, I sat on a fence in the hot Arkansas sun, watching Ringling Brothers Circus come to town.

My folks were preachers, with warm hearts and a simple Christ-exalting Gospel. We had an old ragged tent for some of our meetings, nothing like the one I saw going up that day. Money was scarce. There were no dimes for a circus. And my folks were strict too. Even if we had had the money, we wouldn't have been allowed to go to the Big Show. But Mom and Dad said I could go down to see the elephants and hear the men shout and strain as they pulled the ropes to raise the "Big Top" high in the air.

That dusty summer afternoon I watched the people rush to the entrance. I clutched my fists and said to myself, "If God had a tent like that, He'd have a crowd like that!"

Ever since that day, I've never wanted to see God's work put in some dingy back alley. I think the Lord deserves the best. If people are going to find Jesus Christ, their only hope of salvation ... if we are to do what God told us to do to rescue the lost for Him ... we've got to put God on Main Street.

R.E.H.

Ab|H467

"I know thy works: behold, I have set before thee an open door, and no man can shut it: for thou hast a little strength, and hast kept My Word, and hast not denied My Name." (Revelation 3:8)

CHAPTER 1

It is Sunday morning. I have only a few moments before the Sunday worship service—moments to share with God, as I always do.

But today is different. This morning the *Akron Beacon Journal* of July 26, 1970, lies on my desk. Tears misted my eyes as I read the story written by Peter Geiger for today's edition. He tells WHAT happened here.

He tells, in detail, what Jim Bishop summed up in his column recently: "**Today, his [Rex Humbard's] hour-long service is syndicated to 225 television stations from coast to coast—and deep into Canada. It is, by far, the biggest one-man crusade for Christ in the world. The audience numbers about 15,000,000.**"

Here is Peter Geiger's account of "what happened."

The Congregation Is Continental
By Peter Geiger
Beacon Journal Religious Writer

Inside the huge, circular Cathedral of Tomorrow, a congregation of more than 3,000 worshippers is bowed in silent prayer.

They wait for the pastor's "amen." It never comes.

Instead, banks of twelve 10,000-watt kleig lights flare up, flooding $100,000 worth of crimson velour drapes with blinding light.

The congregation looks up from the prayer in awe as a glissando of chimes fills the auditorium with sound.

A huge cross, hung horizontally from the ceiling, blazes in three alternating colors supplied by 72,000 light bulbs.

Four color television cameras play on the curtains, which rise to reveal a 48-voice choir in two ranks, along with an orchestra of three guitarists, a violinist, pianist and female marimba player.

Their music is as amplified as it is familiar: "This is my story, this is my song: Praising my Savior all the day long."

But newcomers soon know the worship service is unlike any they have ever attended before.

Indeed rather than merely a worship service, it is a full-fledged, professionally competent television show.

There follows a fast-paced melange of mountain-flavored gospel songs by such performers as the Rev. Rex Emanuel Humbard and his wife, Maude Aimee; Johnny Hope, the singing public relations man, and the Golden Triplets, three blondes who dress in yellow.

It is punctuated by a 20-minute sermon from Mr. Humbard in a simple, forceful manner.

The televised portion is wrapped up by the Rev. C. Wayne Jones, associate pastor and Mr. Humbard's brother-in-law, speaking to a camera offstage.

Mr. Humbard, now off camera, used the same moments for making church announcements, receiving new members and other, purely local business.

Videotapes of the service, meanwhile, are duplicated and sent, two weeks later, to 242 stations across the North American continent. That's 44 stations more than carry the Ed Sullivan's Show, network TV's most widespread program.

The cost is $4.3 million a year.

The Cathedral of Tomorrow presents a striking appearance as a church edifice with its steel, glass and marble, but Mr.

Humbard shrugs off any claim for its magnificence.

"It might just as well be filled with hay," he said. "My job is to get people right with God, not to build round cathedrals or buy television equipment. Those are just the tools we use."

Those tools have prodigious effect.

Circulation of the Cathedral's magazine, "The Answer," is approaching a half-million monthly. It is sent to everyone who mails in a contribution.

The contributions pay the total television bill, leaving the local congregation with only a $500,000 annual bill for education and visiting ministers plus other local activities. TV also pays for half the mortgage and maintenance costs of the cathedral building.

"I am television pastor to hundreds of thousands of folks all over the U.S. and Canada, some of whom never get to church," Mr. Humbard says.

Television viewers pay for Mr. Humbard's weekly flights in the Cathedral's four-engine, jet-prop Viscount to one-night stands in cities across the continent.

Mr. Jones, former motorcycle racer and World War II fighter pilot, alternates with full-time airman Merrill Schar at the controls. The "TV staff" of a dozen on-camera regulars accompanies them.

Local pastors approve of the Cathedral team's visits to their cities because the TV pastor always tells his flock to go to their local churches.

Yet, Mr. Humbard and his co-workers haven't overlooked their 3,000-member local flock.

They are engaged in the work of personal salvation, not social action. Their effect on the community is indirect. But in some ways, the effect can be measured by the lives of the church members.

"I stand on that platform Sunday mornings and see changed lives before me," Mr. Jones contends. "There will be a dozen families which, when I met them, were in an hour of crisis. Now they are assets to the community, not liabilities.

"For instance, there is one man and wife who were members of a motorcycle gang. They were headed for divorce. One day they happened to see Rex on TV interviewing a happy family. They liked what they saw.

"They came to the Cathedral and heard the Gospel. They accepted Jesus Christ as their Savior and, from that moment, their lives started to show a change. Now, 10 years later, each of them teaches Sunday School and they have a wonderful, happy family. This is what the Gospel is all about."

Mrs. Ellen Olson, a resident of the Cathedral Apartments, the church's housing project for the elderly, came here from Phoenix to be closer to her family in Western Pennsylvania and also to be next door to her TV preacher.

"I like every bit of this ministry," she remarks. "I go to every service that I can."

Mrs. Olson gets a special satisfaction out of the adult Sunday School class taught by Mr. Jones.

"He's terrific," she declares.

The Cathedral in Cuyahoga Falls arose from a troubled background in Akron.

Mr. Humbard was born in 1919 in Little Rock, Ark., the oldest of six children. His father, A.E. "Dad" Humbard, later became the pastor of the Hot Springs, Ark., Gospel Temple.

Rex graduated from Hot Springs High School, but has no further, formal education.

"I just grew up in the ministry," he explains. He was ordained in his father's church.

Rex came to Akron for the first time in 1952, advance man for his father's troupe of family evangelists. He liked the place immediately.

"Dad" Humbard and the Hot Springs group set its tent at Municipal Airport and drew SRO crowds through most of its Summer stand.

When the team moved on to Cleveland, Rex recognized Akron faces in the nightly audiences. He decided he had found a home in Akron.

He came back here when the family went south for the Winter. With his wife Maude Aimee and brother Clement, he began services in a closed Copley rd. motion picture house and also started a series of radio programs.

Clement did not stay. He returned south and later came to Youngstown to build a circular church patterned after his big brother's Cathedral.

In 1953, Mr. Humbard and his growing congregation moved to the larger Ohio Theater on State rd. in Cuyahoga Falls and re-named it Calvary Temple. It was from this base that plans were laid for erecting a church at Portage Trail and State rd., site of the present Cathedral.

Those plans fell through for lack of financing. Something even grander was in the offing, however.

Acting as his own contractor, Mr. Humbard began in 1957 to build the circular edifice with 5,000 theater seats on the ground which had previously been broken.

Almost from the beginning he was plagued with money woes. The construction loan was not adequate to cover all the added expenses caused by wage and price increases and last minute changes to the plans. The builders and lending instutitions began to clamor for payments.

Mr. Humbard was able to balance the demands for five years. In the process, the Cathedral got a bad name for money management and Mr. Humbard acquired a distaste for talking about his finances.

Rescue came in 1963 when the Teamsters Union Ohio Pension Fund gave the Cathedral a mortgage for $1.2 million—about $750,000 less than the construction cost.

The new mortgage lowered monthly payments to $10,453 including 6.5 pct. interest—about half the former rates. That ended high payments to builders and put the building fund on a basis that church members could handle.

Said Mr. Humbard at the time in regard to the source of the financing, "My interest was in getting the loan, not the place from which it came."

Meanwhile, the Cathedral was collecting rent for a separate

building erected on the south side of its parking lot. It was leased to Shoppers Fair, a discount department store.

Last year, the Shoppers Fair lease was cancelled. The building sat vacant longer than anyone intended, but in June the Cathedral announced a $3 million expansion program which will include use of the structure.

It will house WCOT-TV, the Cathedral's long-awaited UHF television station on Channel 55 plus TV production studios for the Cathedral program and for rent to other TV producers.

There will also be a restaurant on the ground floor, and on a previous-unused lower level, a number of Sunday School classrooms. That will relieve overcrowding in the Cathedral, where some classes currently meet in hallways.

Plans also show the former Shoppers Fair structure linked to the Cathedral by an enclosed, above-ground walkway. At its mid-point is a 250-seat circular chapel.

The project will be financed by an extension of the Teamsters mortgage.

Last year, construction was completed on Cathedral Apartments, a $2.5 million, 13-story building for the elderly. Federally financed and sponsored by the church, it contains 202 apartment units.

It is located on Cathedral property behind the former Shoppers Fair building, but there is no church membership requirement for rental. That is according to federal regulations.

Physical expansion of the Cathedral of Tomorrow reflects a burgeoning program. As the institution recovered its wind following some of the roundhouse blows it has sustained, the ministerial staff has gradually been expanded.

The Cathedral is $400,000 behind its 1970 budget income, but Mr. Humbard seems content.

That is because the shortage is intentional for a change. It is due to a gamble Mr. Humbard has taken over the past 18 months to add nearly 100 television stations carrying weekly services from the Cathedral.

The TV preacher has confidence that income from viewers

in the new cities will cover the increased costs.

"They don't pay right away, of course," Mr. Humbard explains. "Sometimes we have to carry an area for as much as two years. But this is the Lord's work and whatever is required we'll do it to the best of our ability."

The ability of the Cathedral to engage in creative, deficit financing is something relatively new, though Mr. Humbard has always had confidence that his day would come. Even in his darkest hours he had enthusiasm that, in anyone else, would have been thought irrational.

"An ordinary man would have rolled over and died," he says. "I had the Lord on my side."

Says Mr. Jones: "You haven't seen anything yet. We're just getting started."

But now, in these moments of quiet, I keep thinking I want people to know—not just WHAT has happened here—but HOW it has come about.

It started so long ago.

First, there was an idea—a dream to send the Gospel throughout all the United States and around the world.

It began with $65—all that I had in the world.

But most of all, it started with God.

"God is the Answer"—and it is around Him that the Cathedral of Tomorrow centers. He is the One Who touched my heart and made me a new creature, washed in the Blood of the Crucified Lamb. He is the One Who led me, giving me lessons all along the way. Lessons I didn't even know I needed and sometimes didn't want to learn! He is the One Who tested my faith—and increased it.

Let me tell you HOW. . .

"Train up a child in the way he should go: and when he is old, he will not depart from it." (Proverbs 22:6)

CHAPTER 2

I have never doubted God's touch on my life.

I love life itself—the fresh promise of each new day. I love people. I never tire of talking with them, of shaking their hands and sharing their problems. But most of all, I love the Lord. My relationship to Him is not big and mysterious. It is as natural to me as breathing. I cannot imagine one day apart from Him. I know I am nothing without the Lord.

I was born August 13, 1919, at Little Rock, Arkansas. The first words I recall were the prayers of my parents. They were both evangelists back in the days when men of God lived by faith and showed it. They named me Alpha Rex Emmanuel Humbard, the first name after my father. My mother often tells of how she took me in her arms when I was two days old and committed me to God's service. "Rex," she instructed, "you are God's child. You are to be used of the Lord and you are not to go off after the world. If you do, sooner or later you'll get into trouble. You are to stay close to God and listen to what God has to say and do what He tells you in His Word, from beginning to end."

Having a small baby with them didn't interfere with their preaching the Gospel. Each night I was brought to the service. When I was old enough to walk, a pallet was made up on the platform behind the piano, and I fell asleep to the

Gospel music and the thunderous preaching of my father. Discipline was strict. Dad and Mom had traveled for years, living in the homes of others and observing the way parents brought up their children. Now they were determined that their children would not be spoiled. I uttered no protest when, before the service, my father would lay his fingers over my closing eyelids and say, "Now go to sleep and don't you move until after the service." Evidently only the first two or three times was I restless, and after that I was used to it and uttered no protest. Surprisingly, many latecomers never suspected my parents had a child there.

Only once, when I was old enough to toddle around, did my behavior provide an object lesson for the congregation. In a big meeting in Webb City, Missouri, my father was bothered by a couple of little girls who were allowed to run in and out of the aisles during the service. Not wanting to hurt the feelings of their mothers, yet eager to protect the spirit of his meetings, he prayed he'd find the right way to handle the reprimand. Dad told it this way: "At that time we were staying in the home of a couple who also had only one child, and she was allowed to do as she pleased. Rex was permitted to play with her during the day since they both were about the same age, but we kept a tight rein on him.

"One night at the church Rex was in his usual place behind the piano, supposedly asleep. During the preliminaries I heard footsteps pattering across the stage and I looked around. It was this little girl. She went over, punched Rex and then ran off to try to get him to chase her. Rex rose on one elbow and looked at her and then looked over at me. But as the song service progressed, I guess I forgot about him. Just before I began to preach, I heard four little feet, instead of two, go across the stage. Rex hadn't been able to stand it any longer and had taken out after her. I said to myself, 'Well, Lord, perhaps this is my chance to preach on raising children right.'

"I picked up Rex and laid him across the pulpit for a good spanking and then set him down. I didn't have to tell him where to go. He beat it back to the pallet, put his finger in his mouth and went to sleep. That is the last time that ever happened. Then I took my text. 'Train up a child in the way he should go: and when he is old, he will not depart from it.' "

Dad later told me the whole church was packed out that night and the people—including those two families who had children making trouble—took it as a lesson to take their own children in charge. From then on, there were no more disturbances.

Believing God's Word was the basis of my home training. I was never tempted to doubt that if God said it, it was so. Mom likes to tell of the time when my father was entertaining a visiting preacher, Brother Snider, in his tabernacle at Pangburn, Arkansas. About two and a half miles away was a well known cliff called Hiram Bluff. Brother Snider asked if we could go out there to see it, and so we rode the buggy out to the bluff. Mom held tightly to my hand. I was only a little over two, and she thought my curiosity might draw me too close to danger.

As we stood there looking out over the surrounding countryside, Brother Snider called me. Mom reluctantly released my hand to let me scamper over to him. The preacher inquired, "Look out there, little Rex. What do you see?"

"A bluff."

"Yep, isn't that great!" Then he added, "Youngster, who d'ya think made that bluff?"

Mom said I backed up and looked puzzled. I appeared amazed at the ignorance of this man, but I looked him right in the eye and declared loudly, "God said, 'Let there be bluff,' and there was bluff."

We always had a family altar in our home. From babyhood on I was taught the story of the King of Kings. And we literally lived by faith. Money wasn't plentiful in that part of the country; food was scarce at times. I remember Mom's answer to the news that there was nothing to eat. "Get out the pans and then we'll pray. God has never let us down yet." And He never did.

We were poor by men's standards. . .but we were rich in the presence of God. We knew how to take God at His Word. Mom and Dad preached Bible religion—just taking the Bible as it is. They didn't try to change it or overemphasize one part and neglect another. Dad once had been a farm boy, tongue-tied and without much formal education. But he managed to acquire a Bible and took it with him to the fields where he could study as he worked. There as a young lad he heard the command of God, "Take up thy cross and follow Me." Thousands of souls won to the Saviour was the harvest that came from that decision.

Born in Chillicothe, Missouri, my mother, Martha Bell Childers, lost her mother when she was only eight months old. She and her five brothers and sisters traveled with their father by covered wagon from Missouri to Arkansas. There one night the family attended a meeting held by a woman from St. Louis known as Mother Barnes. They heard the testimony of this former Catholic lady who had never touched a Bible until she was 27 years old and then found Christ during a revival in a little Methodist church. Deeply moved by her story, twelve-year-old Martha and her family, with the exception of one brother, yielded their hearts to Jesus Christ and pledged themselves to winning others. Her father felt God's call to the ministry and remained a great preacher until the day God called him Home. Martha gave herself to the work of the ministry and traveled as an assistant to the evangelist Mother Barnes until her own marriage.

When Martha Bell Childers and Alpha E. Humbard met at a preaching convention in Eureka Springs, Arkansas, each knew this was God's choice for his life's partner, despite the fact they barely spoke that first time and they were not to see each other again for a full year. United in the Lord, finally, their years of service together brought joy and blessing. They were always on the move. They never accumulated much of this world's goods. One time when the children were small, Dad told Mom, "I used to yearn to be able to leave the youngsters something, but God spoke to me and said, 'I've not called you to build houses. I've called you to build character.' "

I was the oldest of six children. My sister Ruth was born a year and a half after I was, and then followed Clement, Leona, Mary and Juanita. In the twenty-five years my mother and father reared us, they were continuously in Gospel work, traveling in many states and Canada. Dad pioneered and built many churches. He was simple and down-to-earth, an old-fashioned country preacher. He believed the inspired Word of God and preached it with power. Mother was the one who had the faith. If we kids needed a pair of shoes or if we didn't have food on the table (and there were a lot of times like that during the depression), it was Mom who would go down the hall, close the door and start praying. If we had a need we would always tell her; and when she went to that bedroom to pray, we knew something would happen. Mom never missed more than a few night services in all those years with Dad. She did all her own work, yet never failed to pray at least an hour each day. Both of my parents gave us the greatest heritage we could ever have—a heritage of sincere dedication to the Lord's work and a faith in God. They taught us to live for the Lord and to trust Him.

Music was Dad Humbard's prescription for idleness in children. He believed in the old adage, "Idleness is the devil's workshop," and promptly ruled that a musical education was essential for his growing youngsters. Dad had always been a great lover of music. Regretfully, he felt the lack of musical training in his own ministry. To purchase new instruments for us was out of the question, but a pawn shop provided ones that Dad could afford at a dollar down and a dollar a week. There were two mandolins for the girls, a guitar for me, a banjo for Clement, and a piano accordion for Mom, which Ruth promptly took over and started to play. Soon the house resounded with noise from every room. Now the problem was how to turn all that noise to real music. Dad and Mom prayed.

A few days later a man knocked on the door and introduced himself. "How do you do, preacher. My name's Oscar Chilton. I'm a bit down on my luck, and I thought you might help me out, 'cause I understand larger crowds come to your church than to any other church in the county. I was a music teacher in Chicago, and I want to get into some church with my family. I'd play the music for the privilege of announcing for some students. I just need to get some work and get something to eat for my family."

Dad knew the Lord had answered his prayer, and that Sunday Mr. Chilton and his two children played for the singing. Five or six pupils responded with requests for music lessons after Mr. Chilton made his announcement. At the end of the service, however, Dad discovered the man had rented a house nearby for ten dollars a month but was afraid he wouldn't be able to meet the payments immediately.

"I'll tell you what I'll do," Dad countered. "I have plenty of rooms here over the church where my family is living." His eyes twinkled as he talked. "I'll give you and your family a place to live with all utilities furnished if you'll agree to give my family music lessons."

The deal was arranged and all of us started studying music. Clement, Ruth and Leona worked hard since the teacher was excellent, a real perfectionist. To those three it wasn't drudgery; it was fun. But I was thirteen, old enough to know that if I learned to play I'd have to play every night at church. I wasn't about to do that! Shy as I was, I dragged along, making a pretense of interest until the third lesson.

Mr. Chilton grew more and more nervous and impatient until suddenly he lost his temper completely and shouted to Dad, "I'm going to throw this boy and his guitar right out that window if you don't get him out of here."

"Now, what's the matter here?" Dad asked, looking at me sternly after Mr. Chilton's outburst.

"I can't teach him when he just sits there biting his fingernail and staring out the window," the music teacher steamed.

I protested. "Dad, none of the Humbards is musical. I've been with you up to those family reunions in Muncie, Indiana and Cleveland, Tennessee. None of the Humbards is good at music. It's just not in a Humbard, that's all!"

The silence was painful. Then Dad said slowly, "Well, it's in one of them."

"Who?" I inquired, startled by that news.

"You." And with that he got out a switch.

Three months later, when the teacher packed up his family and started off to Texas, Ruth and Leona and Clement had already reached the point where they could study profitably on their own. I might have known that my father's hopes and prayers for me would only make him more determined. He issued an ultimatum. "I'll give you just 30 days to learn to play that guitar well enough to join the others on the platform for the services."

Stubbornly, I let the days pass by, but soon the dreaded Sunday night arrived. With the church packed, I found myself on the front row, guitar in hand, barely knowing one note from another. Perspiration rolled on my brow and crept down the back of my neck. I sat there, trying to avoid everyone's eyes, choking with embarrassment. That guitar felt like a load of cement. I couldn't play a note.

Then one night things changed. Sitting in a night service, listening to a visiting evangelist preach, I knew God was speaking to me. It was all suddenly different. I had been brought up in church. I went to services just about every night. My folks were what most people would label "religious." But right then I knew I had to make my own decision. The church or even my parents couldn't determine my standing with God. When the preacher gave the altar call and the music started, I felt a small voice calling me to go forward to claim Jesus Christ as my Saviour and Lord. I hesitated. Evidently the Lord knew I needed a little push because a Christian woman stepped across the aisle to ask me quietly, "Are you saved?"

Right then I stepped out and walked down that aisle to kneel at the altar and open my heart to Jesus Christ. Light flooded my soul and I became a new person. Now I really wanted to live for the Lord. In that moment God took my old shyness away and made me an extrovert. He started me talking about Him and I haven't been able to stop since. From that night on, I was likely to be the one in our meetings to jump up and testify for the Lord, a thing which had always before embarrassed me to see people do. The Lord had changed my heart and made me over.

The very next Sunday night came around and my attitude about music had reversed. I watched the person beside me as he played. I took in everything, checking his fingers in each position on the guitar. During the following week I bought a chord book and practiced for hours. The following Sunday night I was beginning to plunk away. With heightened interest and concentration—which is what I'd been lacking all those weeks with the teacher—and with all the zeal of a brand new Christian, I made up my mind to learn. The next day I trudged over to the local radio station to watch a band perform, and each day afterwards I learned my chords by watching them play and then going back home to try the same techniques. Dad's prayers were answered. In my desperation I had grown interested and was practicing hard.

Clem and the girls joined me for practice sessions, and together we worked till we sounded pretty good. To add to the reality, I placed a music stand in front of us and told them it was a microphone. "We need to learn to be professional," I reasoned, as we pretended we were playing and singing for a radio audience.

Though our zeal was hard to live with, my folks never complained. Many days we practiced until 2:30 in the morning. One time, not able to sleep, Mom begged Dad to go shoo the children to bed so they could get some rest.

"No," responded my father, "we had too hard a time getting them started. I'm not going to do anything to interfere now!"

The local radio station, KTHS, had a two-hour Saturday night program known as "The Saturday Night Jamboree," originating from the City Auditorium in Hot Springs. One day I went down and talked with the station manager about letting the Humbard group appear on the program for one number, and they agreed. That night fifteen different groups performed and we ended up playing one religious song. When the red light flashed off, indicating the broadcast was over, several of the station personnel rushed up to scold us, insisting religious music wasn't appropriate on that program. A little disheartened, we went home and turned the matter over to the Lord. The next week, to our surprise, we were invited to return. The station had been bombarded with 85 letters, 65 of which specifically complimented the Humbard group on their music and requested more religious numbers on return engagements. Soon we became a regular feature and the program gradually took on a greater balance of religious music than secular. The title of the show was changed to "The Country Store." Eventually, we were given our own Saturday morning program each week over the same station.

Shortly after this, a talent scout from WLS Barn Dance in Chicago came to Hot Springs and offered the four of us $100 each, per week, to appear in Chicago on the program, plus additional income for road shows. That was big money for those days.

"What would we have to do?" I asked, suddenly wary.

"Well, I guess you can play and sing what you've been doing here—but naturally we'd expect some hillbilly and secular numbers mixed in. I've got to hand it to you kids. With that variety, you'll be a great road show unit."

Gravely I explained we were interested only in spreading the Gospel through our music. We'd have to turn the offer down. The man from Chicago seemed disgusted. "You'll never go anywhere without mixing it up."

"Look, mister, more people like Gospel music than you think," I argued. "I'm sure we'll go somewhere with our Gospel songs. The Lord isn't going to let us down."

That man must have been impressed, for the next Sunday night at church I looked down and, to my amazement, saw him in the second row. After church he introduced himself to my father, saying he had to meet the parents of a boy who would refuse that kind of money because of a conviction in his own heart. "I admit this is the first church I've attended in over 30 years. You've got to have something here. I thought just about everybody put money first and everything else afterward these days."

During those years we were kept busy playing and singing, first for church services and radio programs and eventually also for local events and concerts. Everyone seemed to enjoy our music, perhaps because we sincerely believed in the message of Jesus Christ which we were telling and loved to give out the stories of God's Word. Sometimes we found it a bit difficult to sandwich in our school between the radio broadcasts and church meetings, but somehow the Lord worked it all out. In the summer when school vacations rolled around, the whole family packed up to travel all over the country, holding meetings wherever the Spirit of God led us. Those were times of great blessing and abundant fruit for the Lord.

While we were in Hot Springs in January, 1939, we were invited by V.O. Stamps of the Stamps-Baxter Music and Printing Company to go to Dallas where he was arranging a March of Dimes Benefit program for the President's birthday celebration. It was to be held in the Fair Park Auditorium at the State Fair Grounds of Dallas. Already he had called in singers and musicians from all over the country for the special event. We Humbards were delighted to be included in the invitation.

What a great night that was for me! Striding toward me came Reverend Albert Ott, the dynamic pastor of Bethel Temple of Dallas, a man I'd long heard of and admired. "Look, son," he began, "I'm impressed with the talent of your group. What about appearing on our church radio program tomorrow morning?"

I quickly assented, and the next morning when we arrived, we discovered Reverend Ott and V.O. Stamps had been conferring and had agreed on a plan to keep the Humbard family busy in Dallas for at least the next thirteen months. Brother Ott explained that he, as pastor of Bethel Temple—a church with more than a thousand on the Sunday School roll, had at least thirteen radio broadcasts each week. He suggested we work in his church, appearing on all broadcasts, while at the same time helping Mr. Stamps with his radio schedule and in concerts and musical programs in a 500 mile radius of Dallas. To four naive country kids, that was an offer! While we had yearned to declare God's power and love, in song and story, God had been arranging it beyond our greatest expectations.

Financial details were incidental to us. We wanted to gain experience and sing for the Lord. But God provided for our needs. In exchange for Mom and Dad and all the children working in the church and appearing on the thirteen programs per week, Reverend Ott offered $37.50 a week spending money for the entire family, plus rooms in which to live. V.O. Stamps said he'd add an additional $25 per concert and provide us a car. To our joy, topping off the offer, he also promised to supply free music lessons for us in either of his two music schools.

With mounting enthusiasm and with this further assurance of God's leading, we then also found it possible to attend Adamson High School in Dallas. We were given special permission to arrive late each morning so we could regularly appear on early morning broadcasts. Every obstacle to God's will for us seemed swept away. There was no doubt that God was guiding us each step. Those weeks and months were jammed with activity. Usually we appeared on as many as 28 radio broadcasts per week, plus attending the two Sunday services and a Wednesday service at Bethel Temple. In addition to these, days were filled with our musical studies and school work. Free moments were absorbed by those trips from 50 to 500 miles away for Mr. Stamps. I sometimes wondered when we ever found time to sleep.

Amid all these activities, somehow I managed to get my diploma from high school that year. Before I went to Dallas I had just about completed my work, except for a few credits. When Commencement time rolled around, I received my diploma from the high school in Hot Springs (where my name was read and a blank diploma was awarded) but the real diploma was presented at Adamson High School in Dallas. With the name "Rex Humbard" being called out in two high schools on the same night, I still managed to miss walking down an aisle in academic robe and tasseled cap, for I was with the Stamps Quartet miles away playing for an audience of 8,000 people. Nothing was ever allowed to interfere with the Lord's work.

Our trip to Dallas to the President's March of Dimes Benefit was memorable to me for another reason. I had already recognized God's guidance in opening up a tremendous new area of service. But I had yet to realize there was someone I met that night who would become unforgettable.

"And the Lord God said, It is not good that the man should be alone: I will make him an help meet for him." (Genesis 2:18)

CHAPTER 3

Standing backstage at the State Fairgrounds Auditorium that night in 1939, I glanced up to meet the most penetrating gaze I'd ever seen. I caught my breath and decided to amble over to speak to this girl. I barely noticed the other two girls there; obviously all were members of a trio. Somehow there came to my mind something to say. "If you're not going out on stage right away, would you mind keeping an eye on my baby sister while we sing our number?"

"I'd be glad to," came her quick answer, and then I found myself steering her over toward little three-year-old Juanita and dashing after my family who were then going out on stage. At least I knew she'd be there when I returned.

Memories of that evening flash back to both of us. Reverend Albert Ott, her pastor, was pleased with the number "The Meeting In the Air," which we'd just played and sung. He had hurried backstage to tell me of his plans for us. Once there, he noticed me standing beside one of his parishioners, and promptly he formally introduced me to Maude Aimee Jones, and then added, "I'm delighted to tell you Rex and his family may be joining our radio staff at Bethel Temple—that is, if I can persuade him now."

When my family returned to Dallas, one month later, we began our work which was to keep us there for two full years. Several weeks after our arrival, I was invited to a young people's Valentine party, sponsored by the church and held in the Y.W.C.A. As soon as I arrived, I noticed Maude Aimee and made sure I got the seat next to her. During part of the program I serenaded her with the song "I Want a Girl Just Like the Girl That Married Dear Old Dad." When she smiled, I felt exactly as I had the day back in Little Rock when I won the award for pole vaulting. Suddenly, I was on top of the world.

They say an Arkansas Traveler is slow, and Maude Aimee soon discovered I was no exception. It took six months before we were "officially" going together. She was fifteen and I was eighteen. On the day I was graduated from high school, she presented me with a box tied with bright ribbons. I remember fumbling with it, more conscious of her eyes and laughter than of what I was doing. The tie and the shirt I found in that package I can still describe, and to this day Maude Aimee has the tie—a bit tattered and torn, perhaps, but reminding her of our excitement that night.

Maude Aimee's mother was an old-fashioned Christian and was even more strict, in guidance, because there was no father in the home. She had been a widow since the time her little girl was fifteen months old. When I asked permission to take her daughter to her first football game at the Cotton Bowl, she agreed, but solely for the reason I was a Christian young man. I couldn't mask my admiration for this woman who had reared a tiny girl and her fast-growing older brother in the fear of the Lord. I loved to hear her talk about those days.

Fondly she told of the day, May 22, 1922, when God sent this lively baby girl into their home. Her black hair and snapping black eyes contrasted with alabaster white skin, causing considerable comment. It was not until she grew a bit older and demonstrated an intense personality that one visiting preacher teasingly dubbed her "The Master Mind."

She had persistent curiosity about everything. It wasn't enough to tell her something was so. One had to tell her why. Like most children, she had her mischievous moments, but her well-educated conscience usually prompted her to crawl under the bed to hide until her deed was discovered and time for punishment arrived. As a child, she rarely cried, seemed easy to reason with and displayed an understanding beyond her years.

Being a godly mother, Mrs. Maude Jones had named her daughter after the evangelist Aimee Semple McPherson, praying earnestly that God would grant her little girl grace to love the Lord and zeal to become a soul-winner. Fortunately, the Christian atmosphere of their home was heightened by many visits of ministers. Almost every great man of God who came to that area for revivals would come to their house for dinner and conversation.

Maude Aimee found Christ as her personal Saviour at the age of six, a tribute to her mother's faithfulness and her attendance at a church where the Gospel was clearly preached so even a child could understand. One Sunday night when Reverend Ott preached, he ended the service by asking if there was anyone present who knew the Lord as Saviour and wanted to be baptized—who, right then, would come forward. God spoke to her heart. She was ready to obey Him. Only later did she remember she was wearing her favorite frilly dress—one for which she had begged her mother for months. God's blessing overshadowed all disappointment.

At an early age Maude Aimee discovered she had a voice—not just an ordinary one, but a voice that must be a gift from God. Her mother taught her that, with this blessing, there was also a responsibility. Consequently, at the age of five, Maude Aimee performed on the radio every Saturday, singing heartily the story of Jesus. When she was eight, she began to sing at most of the Sunday church meetings, as well as in nightly revival services, whenever it was possible. As she grew older, her life differed greatly from those of her schoolmates. She found her happiness, not in attending shows and dances, but in serving the Lord with the gift God had bestowed. And there was plenty of opportunity at Bethel Temple. At that time it was the largest Assembly of God church in the United States.

Reaching the age of sixteen, Maude Aimee went to work as a window dresser for women's fashions at a large department store in Dallas and continued there until she married. Despite my efforts, that marriage seemed to be continually postponed.

I have no doubt I was probably the most enthusiastic suitor in all of Dallas. Each morning as soon as I signed off the radio program, I'd call her; and then at 4:15 each afternoon I'd race to her house and stay 'til church. The courtship was hard on Maude Aimee's mother, for we were carefully chaperoned every minute—even out on dates. Occasionally Mrs. Jones would get so tired she'd announce, "Time's up!" I'd reluctantly leave. Maude Aimee and I didn't object, really. Now, we look back to that time and, remembering her standards, thank God for her.

V.O. Stamps observed us together a great deal, since we frequently appeared on the same radio broadcasts. Once I overheard his comment, "Those two are just meant for each other." Maybe this is what prodded me to come to a decision. Our backgrounds, our home training, our love for the Lord and His service were so similar that I knew our future goals would be the same, as well. On December 19, 1939, I popped the question.

"Maude Aimee," I began, "I need you for my life-partner." And then, desperately, I added, "In fact, I've just got to have you."

Probably I would have gone on and on in my awkward eagerness, except right then Maude Aimee startled me with a simple reply. "O.K., Rex."

On Christmas Eve, I showed up with a huge box, three feet square, beautifully gift-wrapped. She untied it and, surprised, discovered another. And then another. And then another and another until finally she came to a box about the size of a fifty-cent piece. Inside this was a note saying, "Look in the other box." Now, thoroughly puzzled, she glanced up to see me pulling a jeweler's box out of my pocket. Here was her engagement ring.

As I placed it on her finger, we pledged our love to each other and to the Lord. Two happier young people couldn't have been found anywhere. We believed God, in His infinite love, was smiling down on us. And, together, with Him, we felt nothing would ever go wrong.

"And we know that all things work together for good to them that love God, to them who are the called according to His purpose." (Romans 8:28)

CHAPTER 4

The good Lord in His wisdom knows when we are ready to receive the blessings prepared for us. And the old saying "The course of true love never runs smooth" was as true for us as for scores of others since the beginning of time.

Maude Aimee's mother and my parents were devoted to the Word of God and lived by it. Consequently, they felt marriage should never be entered into lightly. Maude Aimee was only seventeen years old and I was twenty. Naturally it was felt we were both still too young to bear the great responsibilities of marriage. Talking it over together with our parents, we realized the wisdom of becoming more firmly established in our life's work, since God had called us into His service. We loved the Lord so much we wanted to put Him first in everything.

Shortly before this time, the Lord had opened a new work for the Humbard family in Little Rock, Arkansas. It meant a prolonged separation for Maude Aimee and me—a time to test our love and grow in maturity. Though it almost broke our hearts, we obediently agreed to get along on letters and telephone calls for a year.

The day we left Dallas, I drove the first 85 miles in the wrong gear, my sympathetic family not saying a word. With tears misting my eyes I motored all the way to Little Rock, feeling each turn of the wheels took me farther from the love of my heart.

Then followed months of loneliness which we both tried to fill with letters and phone calls. The postman who delivered Maude Aimee's mail had an extra load to carry those days. Many times there were at least half dozen letters postmarked Little Rock, Arkansas, and I remember one day I managed to write eight letters, one of which was 25 pages long.

I tried to fill my time working long hours. I bought time from radio stations and then secured sponsors to reimburse us. Every morning, seven days a week, our group had a program at 6:15 a.m., which the studios then sent by phone line for airing at 6:45 in Pine Bluff and on to Hot Springs for a 7:15 morning program. By 8 a.m.,the rest of the children were headed off to school and I was busy working on the mail and clearing up business details for our activities.

The mail response from our hour-long Thursday night broadcasts had been overwhelming. The program, running from 11 to 12 p.m., brought mail from 33 states and Canada. At the same time, the Lord was blessing us with revival meetings, tent meetings and services in almost every church or denomination in the city. In addition to all this, every Tuesday night we drove 60 miles for a service in our old home church in Hot Springs. I had assumed the duties of master-of-ceremonies by this time. I managed the arrangements and took charge of altar calls, gaining valuable experience and eventually showing God had given me the ability to encourage people to come to the altar and make a decision to accept Jesus as Saviour.

The nationally known evangelist Jackie Burris began a four-week revival in Robinson Memorial Auditorium in January, 1941. He urged the Humbards to play for the services. Accepting the invitation eagerly, we played for 30 minutes before each meeting. The response to our music was so encouraging to Mr. Burris that when the revival was over, he then asked us to accompany him to his next meeting at Cadle Tabernacle, an auditorium with a capacity of 10,000 in Indianapolis, Indiana.

"Even if it does mean being away from home longer than usual, it's a tremendous opportunity," I suggested to the others when we discussed it.

"And it's a privilege for you youngsters to be a part of such a great meeting," Dad encouraged. "You may as well tell him you'll go, Rex."

The thrilling experience lasted six weeks and the crowds were so large, thousands were turned away. My admiration for Jackie Burris and, most of all, my praise to the Lord knew no bounds. When the meeting was over, we rejoined our parents back in Arkansas and picked up our radio and church ministry which we'd had before.

At first, in these hectic months of work, I had barely noticed Maude Aimee's letters were coming less frequently. Suddenly they dwindled away to an occasional note. Confusion and despair settled over me, but gradually it gave way to confidence that the Lord had a purpose in it and He would work it out to His glory. Months passed. By this time I hadn't heard from Maude Aimee for almost a year.

One day an imposing envelope arrived containing an invitation to a dedication ceremony for a new church in Dallas. My heart gave a leap. Dallas! I answered that invitation immediately, readily accepting. A few days later I was headed toward Dallas with a prayer in my heart. I knew something was going to happen. It had to. I'd see Maude Aimee again.

Memories flashed in my mind. I could remember her sparkle, her very aliveness. I relived our courtship days and my heartbreak in leaving Dallas. What was she doing, I kept thinking. How did she feel? Once again my heart leaped with hope. I felt myself saying the words over and over again, "Lord, direct me. I know You'll never fail me. You, only, know my future. . .and what You want, I want."

In Dallas, Maude Aimee was startled when she heard the news we were coming for the dedication. By this time she was going with another young man, just as I had been dating other girls in recent months. When her boy friend invited her to the dedication service, she accepted, realizing the irony of the situation. She had been thinking of me. Now she knew that when she saw me there, either she'd realize she didn't love me and her imagination had been playing tricks on her, or else she'd know for sure that I was the right one.

As I stood on the platform that night, I looked up to see her being escorted down the aisle. I had always thought she was beautiful, but suddenly I knew I had forgotten what a picture she made. I didn't have a chance. All I could see was that bright red dress contrasting with her black hair and eyes. She had on some kind of rose-trimmed, black straw bonnet, and I remember wondering why all women didn't wear things like that. I couldn't take my eyes off her. I wouldn't have missed her in a crowd of five million.

Normally, as master-of-ceremonies I could be depended upon to keep things running smoothly. But that night I missed some cues, and even Dad could see I was pre-occupied. One thing was clear in my mind. There couldn't be another girl for me—ever. The service closed, and I watched her leave with that young man. I thought I'd lost her.

I spent a restless night, doing more tossing and turning than sleeping. But I prayed, knowing God had the power to do anything. Maude Aimee and I both had felt God would show us His will. God did just that. That night He assured me all over again that prayer changes things. I couldn't see the evidence right then, but I had His answer.

"To everything there is a season, and a time to every purpose under the heaven." God was demonstrating His Word. He must have felt we were ready at last to receive this blessing from Him. I realize that when something comes too easily, we sometimes don't appreciate it or treasure it as we ought. This struggle. . .this heartache. . .made victory even more cherished.

I left Dallas. Three months afterwards, Maude Aimee's mother received a letter from my mother. Mom told her of our current meeting in Indianapolis, at Cadle Tabernacle, and invited Maude Aimee to come up for the last week of her vacation. Mom had added that the family was very eager to have her visit and wanted her to sing for our meeting. Just when the two of them were reading that letter and discussing the wisdom of accepting, the telephone rang.

"Look, Maude Aimee," I started in immediately, "I've got something I've got to discuss with you." I stopped, befuddled, remembering Maude Aimee was not a girl to be begged or coaxed to do anything. If she wanted to do it, she said so. And if not, she'd make that equally clear. She broke in on my thoughts before I could proceed.

"Rex, I'd like to come to Indianapolis to see you and your family. Will you tell your mother and thank her for the letter. I'll take the train tomorrow morning."

I hadn't needed to coax. The Lord was answering my prayers.

The following hours passed as slowly as a year. I met her train and took her on to Cadle Tabernacle just in time to introduce her to the audience and let her sing. Afterwards, we returned to the railroad station to claim her luggage, and on the way home I got to the point right away.

"Are you willing to take up where we left off. . .when we broke our engagement?"

If she was startled by my abruptness, she didn't show it.

She almost surprised me as she answered, "Yes, Rex, I am."

"Will you marry me now? I'm not going to take a chance of losing you again. Maude Aimee, marry me this week."

She smiled slowly. When the answer came, I could barely believe my ears.

"Yes, darling, this week."

"For this cause shall a man leave his father and mother, and shall be joined unto his wife, and they two shall be one flesh." (Ephesians 5:31)

CHAPTER 5

Wedding plans captured our attention. I knew that Maude Aimee—like any other young girl—had looked forward to a big wedding. First I suggested we go back to Dallas and have the ceremony there. But Maude Aimee was too practical for that.

"Rex," she protested, "it would cost more than we can afford to go clear back to Texas. We just don't have that kind of money. . .or even a quarter of what it would take for my dream wedding. We'll just forget about all that."

"But, honey, —"

"No, Rex, I've made up my mind. I'd rather keep what money we have for things we'll need after we're married. Let's ask your dad to marry us in a simple little ceremony."

Our wedding was scheduled for the next Sunday night after the evening service. Dad would officiate, with Ruth and Louis Davidson, my sister and her husband, as our attendants. Because Maude Aimee's mother and brother couldn't possibly make the trip to Indianapolis at that time, we decided it would be best not to tell them our plans until after the wedding was over. I kept thinking Maude Aimee was mighty brave to face all this so far from home, and I wanted to do all I could to compensate for her small wedding.

Small wedding! It turned out to be celebrated by over

8,500 people! I guess I must have sounded mysterious that Sunday night, August 2, 1942, when I made my announcement at the service.

"Folks, there's going to be a wedding immediately after the close of the meeting. If there's anyone who wants to stay, you're welcome."

Perhaps curiosity was the key to the big response, for the auditorium was full when the wedding march began and Maude Aimee entered from the other side of the platform. She looked radiant, more beautiful than I could possibly describe in her light blue dress, as she took her place beside me and Dad led us in our marriage vows.

"Everybody loves a lover" is a saying we often hear, and it surely must be true of Indiana people. The night after the wedding, August 3rd, was the final night of our meetings. Cadle Tabernacle was packed with an enthusiastic crowd. The people who had witnessed the wedding the night before were back. Along with them came hundreds of people who had heard about it and wanted to see the new bride and groom.

Word must have got around how, in all the excitement of the ceremony the night before, I had neglected to kiss my bride. All the ribbing I had taken prompted me to walk out on the platform that Monday evening and declare, "I've been told in all the confusion last night, I forgot to perform one important duty. Since I expect to make this marriage last a lifetime, I certainly want to start it off right. So, I'll try to make amends. May I present the new Mrs. Rex Humbard!"

And amid the blushes of my wife and the laughter of the crowd, I kissed my bride.

After that final service, our car, trimmed with tin cans, proclaimed to the world that we were newlyweds. I carefully drove out of the parking lot, trying to ignore the loud clanking. My embarrassment increased as car after car pulled out behind us to follow down the highway. Honking horns, which heralded our progress all the way down to the business section of town, became far less disturbing to me than the sudden police siren which signaled us to pull over to the curb.

With a feeling of apprehension, I glanced at Maude Aimee and brought the car to a halt, only to see a grinning policeman join in the celebration with the words, "What's the idea of driving without lights? It's a law around here that you use lights after dark."

Then he waved us on. Maude Aimee and I agreed Indianapolis was the friendliest town we'd seen!

Early Wednesday morning we made our way to South Bend, Indiana, where for a brief time we were to make our first home. It was a three-room apartment on the second floor of an old house. Though it was a modest little place, to us it seemed like a palace. Everything in South Bend seemed wonderful. Our meetings were unusually successful, with crowds so large the streets had to be blocked off. People would stand outside the tent and watch the service from there, when they couldn't get inside.

One evening the crowds jammed the tent and God blessed us in a most unusual way. As I was leading the singing, a woman near the back of the tent stood up and started shouting, "I can see! I can see!"

I stopped the music and asked her to explain what she meant. She came forward and gave her testimony. She'd been sitting, listening to the music and praying to herself—enjoying the service even though she couldn't see a thing. She had been totally blind for over sixteen years. As the songs warmed her soul, she said to the Lord, "Oh, Lord, if I could just see the Humbards. . .just see their faces."

No sooner had she prayed with her head bowed, than she noticed the hymnbook in her hands. Looking up in the direction of the platform, she could see light! Finally the haze cleared, and she could see our faces. Her shout of rejoicing and excitement, "I can see! I can see!," brought praise to our hearts. How good God was!

Many people in the audience knew this woman and vouched for the story of her long years of blindness. We were thrilled at this miracle right in our midst, and eventually we saw God bless that meeting with scores of lives being dedicated to Jesus Christ.

While we were in that area, we wanted to drive over to Winona Lake Bible Conference grounds to meet two giants of the faith still in service for the Lord—Mrs. Billy Sunday and Homer Rodeheaver. Here, before their entrance to glory, they carried on the work started by Billy Sunday. What a privilege it was to meet these saints of God, to build our own determination to serve the Lord with the same zeal.

Our meetings in South Bend were closing after that fruitful month. Just before we left, Maude Aimee and I celebrated our first monthly wedding anniversary. I decided to give my lovely young bride a set of silverware to make her feel as if she were a real homemaker. We went out to dinner and exchanged cards, beginning a wonderful tradition in our home. From then on, when the second of each month rolled around, we celebrated our marriage. It brought us closer together. There were many lean months when resources were scarce, but there was always something—a flower, a tiny gift—to show each other our love and our thanks to the Lord for bringing us together. To this day we've followed this custom, and we feel it has made our marriage grow richer and brighter each year. Often I urge couples to observe a similar practice. Perhaps, if they did, all the boredom and dissatisfaction of their marriages would soon disappear.

That fall we planned to have a meeting in Elkhart, Indiana. As we drove over there, we noticed the air felt particularly chilly for September, but we soon forgot about it in the hurry of unloading and settling into a small apartment. I worked with the other men to find a place for the tent and erect it.

Late that night a freak winter storm hit Elkhart—a blizzard so strong it caved in the tent. The snow lay in thick white drifts over the top. There was absolutely no chance of putting the tent to use for the services the next night. We managed to arrange to have services in a local church for the first three nights, and I trusted the Lord would lead us from there.

Certainly I hadn't been expecting cold weather that early. Maude Aimee and Leona watched me shiver around for three days and then finally talked me into driving downtown to a men's clothing store to buy an overcoat. Just as I was deciding on what I wanted, someone slapped me on the back. I twisted around in surprise to face Jack Burris. Laughing at my amazement, he explained he'd been trailing us all over town. He had stopped off on his way to Tulsa to see if we'd go along with him to provide the music for his next big Oklahoma campaign.

Jackie could be very persuasive. "Rex, after all this searching for you, you owe me a 'Yes' answer. How about it?"

I was cautious. "Look, Jackie, we'd love to go, but Tulsa's over a thousand miles away. I guess we'd have to be there by Saturday night and there's hardly time for that. We're already set up here."

"You'll be able to make it. Honestly, I need you, Rex," he pleaded.

We rushed home to repack what we'd just unpacked, and before midnight we were on our way. Lots of hard driving brought us into Tulsa by late Saturday night, and we tumbled into bed, weary, but confident that we were in God's will . . . and that was all that was necessary.

Our blessings were full and running over. The meeting was wonderful. Midway through it, an unexpected surprise arrived. All of us were given three full days of free time. What a present for Maude Aimee! She'd been longing to visit her home. This had been the first time she'd ever been away from her family, and her short trip of one week had stretched into three months. Letters from home spoke glowingly of their happiness for her in her marriage, but her family kept urging her to come home for a few days so they could share in the wedding festivities.

To save time, we decided to fly. Since neither one of us had ever been on an airplane before, we were thrilled. Our excitement mounted when our friends greeted us, en masse, at the Dallas Airport and whirled us away to a combination shower and wedding reception, attended by over two hundred. At last Maude Aimee got her three-tiered wedding cake—almost three months after the actual ceremony. She was equally excited about the lovely gifts. Even when I described the hardships of traveling with so many belongings, she wasn't persuaded to leave anything behind.

"Now, honey," tactfully, I tried to reason with her. "we'll never be able to wedge all that in."

"I love all these pretty things, Rex. I'm going to enjoy them even if I have to sit on them all the way across the country."

All the way back to Tulsa we chuckled about how our wedding itself had been so quiet and hasty, but still we'd managed to stretch the excitement and celebration over three full, wonderful months.

Our meetings resumed. Maude Aimee delighted in her new gifts and trousseau but faced the aggravation of travel-busy days. For example, living in each place for such a short time, she could see laundry presented a serious problem. I'll never forget Maude Aimee's first crisis in washing clothes.

Her new bridal finery was so precious she didn't dare entrust it to a commercial laundry. It piled up until she realized something had to be done. One evening just before leaving for the church service, she grabbed the opportunity to soak her new lingerie in the bathtub, with the intention of handwashing it as soon as she returned. We were invited out after church, and it was early in the morning hours before we got back home, too sleepy to bother about housekeeping pressures. Maude Aimee groaned as she faced the washing, and I talked her into waiting until the next morning before tackling it.

The next day began with a rush to the radio station for our program. Then off we went to a public appearance at the Chamber of Commerce, followed by still more radio programs. Before we knew it, it was time for the evening service again. She thought surely she'd be able to get to the washing that night after the service, but again her plans were foiled. Jackie Burris had scheduled an engagement for us to attend following the meeting. Once again we arrived home past midnight, so tired we could barely move. Again she looked at the clothes in the bathtub and promised herself she would take care of them first thing in the morning.

Sunshine greeted us when we awakened, as well as a peculiar odor. Tracing the smell to the bathtub, Maude Aimee discovered her bridal finery covered with peculiar black spots. Time had run out and mildew had set in!

Despite the little troubles, our stay in Tulsa was a tremendously happy one. The Lord had blessed in the meetings, and we made many wonderful friends. No one can have a better time than a group of Christians who get together in Christian fellowship to love and praise the Lord.

We closed the meeting in Tulsa and packed up to leave. Looking at our luggage, now increased with recently acquired wedding presents, it was apparent to me that even a magician couldn't pack that much into one car. I purchased a little two-wheeled trailer. Even then, it took a lot of ingenuity to get everything loaded before setting out for Little Rock.

It was nearing the Christmas season, the time of the year when traveling evangelists have the leanest period, financially, of all the year. Everyone seems to be too busy getting ready for Christmas celebrations to have revival services. My wife had hoped to spend Christmas in Dallas, but we were scheduled to open a meeting on January 1 in Augusta, Georgia, over a thousand miles away. It was my job to get there early enough to complete arrangements for radio time, newspaper publicity, city permits, personal workers and ushers. All of that took time.

As devoted newlyweds, we decided to leave early and travel alone, spending Christmas on the road heading toward Augusta. We'd never had a honeymoon, so I decided to splurge a little on her Christmas gift. I began the trip by giving her a wristwatch. It was so unexpected that she was delighted. For the next hundred miles, the time of day was more fascinating to her than the scenery along the road. We stopped at Chattanooga, Tennessee, and spent Christmas Eve on top of Lookout Mountain. Just before sundown, we stood gazing out in wonder, over the edge of the mountain, to the seven states visible below. All I could think of was that my Lord owned all that. The world was His, and we shared its treasures as joint-heirs with His Son.

That night we found lodging in a lovely tourist home at the top of the mountain. So gracious was the lady of the house that she served us breakfast on Christmas morning before we set out to travel to Georgia. Perhaps, on that trip, someone might have glimpsed our Arkansas license and felt sorry for the lonely travelers so far from home on Christmas day. Actually, we were joyously happy. We burst out singing as we drove. We were so grateful to God for His love. That day we were celebrating the miraculous birth of His Son, Whose servants we were. And our hearts were full of thanksgiving, too, that the Lord had brought us together. Life was so much fun. Harder times were bound to come. But with God to lean on, we felt nothing would be too hard.

"Now therefore go, and I will be with thy mouth, and teach thee what thou shalt say." (Exodus 4:12)

CHAPTER 6

We arrived in Augusta the day after Christmas. Immediately I set to work making final arrangements for the meeting that was to open New Year's Day. Finding living quarters for a few weeks was the next problem on the list. During these war years, locating an apartment was no easy task. There was nothing available for us in Augusta, but the Lord directed us to a brand new garage apartment, all newly furnished, a few miles away in South Carolina.

As the Augusta meeting began in the new City Auditorium, the Lord continued to pour out His blessing. God worked in those weeks to draw many people to Himself. I remember one man who came forward to claim Jesus Christ as his Saviour. Several days later he was followed by his wife and two of his three children. Though for many years this man had cared nothing about the Lord or religion, now he was concerned for the soul of his one remaining son, who still strayed from God.

With a heavy heart, he confided in me, "I do hope that Oliver, my oldest boy, will give his heart to the Lord before you leave town."

I, too, was burdened for Oliver. I spent a long time praying for him. After the service one night I caught sight of the lad walking ahead of me out of the darkened auditorium.

Impulsively, I caught up to him and asked, "Aren't you ready to give your heart to the Lord?"

Tears began to roll down his cheeks. "I've stood it just as long as I can," he admitted. "I'm ready, Rex."

There in the darkened hall the last of that family became God's child. What rejoicing! The lost sheep of their little flock was now safe in the fold. God not only saved him from sin, but gave him a life of service, for today Oliver is out preaching the Gospel!

One of the greatest rewards connected with the Lord's work is the sight of broken families being reunited. One night a man knelt at one end of the altar, tears streaming down his face. At the other end, a young woman was kneeling, and she too gave her heart to the Saviour. Just as they both stood up, gloriously saved, they happened to see each other. With a cry of joy they ran into each other's arms. They had been a young married couple already in the divorce courts, and now God had made them over and given them a new life in Him. I will never forget them. Certainly they were, to me and to all of Augusta, a testimony of God's ability to patch up broken homes.

Along with the joys connected with serving the Lord, there are countless tragedies to be seen, for often a preacher witnesses the heartache of people who are stubborn and refuse to heed God's call.

One night I was giving an altar call. For the first time I felt impressed to say, "Someone is getting his last call tonight. The Lord is speaking to a person here. You will never again have the opportunity to give your life to God, if you don't do it now. . .tonight!"

I felt an intense burden for that person, and yet I didn't know who it was. Many people streamed down to the altar, but still the burden wasn't lifted. I waited as long as I could, and then I walked down from the stage into the auditorium until I came to a man who was standing near the aisle, crying. Instantly I knew that here was the one God was trying to reach. I stopped and talked to him softly, pleading with him. Obviously God was speaking to him, but still he wouldn't give in.

"Today is the day of salvation," I reminded.

But he just kept repeating, "No. . .no. . .maybe I'll come tomorrow night. . .but not now!"

Finally, God took the burden from me and I mounted the steps of the platform and closed the meeting, remembering God's words given to the prophet Ezekiel: "Yet if thou warn the wicked, and he turn not from his wickedness, nor from his wicked way, he shall die in his iniquity; but thou hast delivered thy soul."

On that same night, a few blocks away from the auditorium, an unknown man slipped out from behind a hedge and attacked this man who had refused God's last call. There in the darkness the assailant robbed him, slit his throat and left him to die. Lost for eternity!

The next revival was in Greenville, South Carolina, and both there and in the previous meeting in Augusta, I did some preaching. I handled the business details for the group, took care of the advance work and advertising, prepared the personal workers and ushers, and performed the duties of master-of-ceremonies. But most of all, I loved to preach. I felt the Holy Spirit leading me each time I opened the Word of God. I hadn't had time to go to a seminary for a formal education for the ministry, but my training had not been totally neglected. Under the guidance of my Heavenly Father, the Greatest of all Teachers, I had been gaining experience. I had grown up in the Lord's work and had assumed responsibilities just as soon as my age permitted it. My brother, Clement, and I were given the opportunity to preach one service each week. Thus we were required to depend on God for our help, and He never let us down.

Now it was decided that I should be ordained. The ordination ceremony was held in the Gospel Tabernacle in Greenville, under the auspices of our home church of Hot Springs, Arkansas, and my license was presented through the International Ministerial Federation, an association of independent ministers. The title, Reverend Rex Humbard, seemed strange to me. Yet I prayed that God's unction would be upon me, and that faithfulness to God would always be the accompaniment to my title.

Like my father, I had long felt I wasn't interested in denominational work. I wanted to preach the Gospel according to God's Holy Word and the dictates of my own conscience. I was disappointed with people and churches who emphasized all kinds of little insignificant differences. I felt all of us could meet at the foot of the Cross of Jesus Christ. Like Paul, I was able to say, "And I, brethren, when I came to you, came not with excellence of speech or of wisdom, declaring unto you the testimony of God. For I determined not to know anything among you, save Jesus Christ, and Him crucified. . .And my speech and my preaching was not with enticing words of man's wisdom, but in demonstration of the spirit and of power: That your faith should not stand in the wisdom of men, but in the power of God."

In preparing for my weekly sermon, I often chose some Bible story to tell which illustrated a great Bible truth. I discovered that God gave me unusual success with these sermon story-illustrations, and it became my favorite method of telling the love of Christ for lost men and women. Many people told me that the Bible stories were clearer and more understandable to them. In hearing this, I thought of the parables of the Son of God, and how those simple comparisons brought wisdom to men's hearts two thousand years ago.

Crowds were flocking to our meetings in Greenville, and I praised God that scores of souls were saved and started on a Christian way of life. It was the first big revival that had been held in Greenville for many years.

Ever since our service in Augusta, Maude Aimee had been ill. Each day she was fighting to keep going, and finally, when she got no better, I insisted it was time she see a doctor. The one she consulted in Augusta suggested she go into a hospital for tests and x-rays. Upon examining the results of these, he told her there was something wrong with her digestive tract. He prescribed more rest and a special diet. She tried to calm down, following his directions carefully; but even when she did, she didn't seem to improve at all.

In Greenville, Maude Aimee decided to try another physician. After two months of suffering, she was still a very sick girl. This time following her examination, the doctor greeted her with twinkling eyes.

"Mrs. Humbard, there's no serious trouble, unless you'd put a new member of the family in that category!"

We were both delighted with his news, and now my wife was quite satisfied with the diagnosis of her condition.

Maude Aimee had always been extremely active in church work, and now with partial rest ordered by the doctor, she felt, as the days passed, that she wasn't doing her part in the services.

"Rex, if I could learn to play some instrument like the rest of you, I'd be much happier. . .and more use to the Lord, too. I've sung ever since I can remember, but now I'd love to be able to play along with the rest of you."

"Honey, you're supposed to take it easy," I protested.

"Well, I don't have to sit around and be completely idle. Rex, please buy me an instrument and teach me to play."

Really, I guess I was secretly pleased.

"Choose any instrument you want, honey."

That was a statement I would live to regret. Maude Aimee promptly chose the vibra-harp, and I bravely went out and bought one.

The first problem was teaching her to play. Her voice—a bell-like, soaring soprano—was a natural gift, and instinctively she knew how to use it. Yet, she had never studied music. Her notes were true and clear, but thanks for that went to God and not to any acquired knowledge. To my surprise, I now discovered my wife didn't know one note from another. She had learned all her music by ear.

I asked her to accompany me to the church one afternoon, and for about an hour I taught her the fundamental chords. That was to be the extent of her music lessons. That night she played right along with the rest of us. So acute was her natural ability that, after practicing during the services every night for a week, she was able to play like a veteran.

The second problem with Maude Aimee's new interest was transportation. The vibra-harp added a great deal to the richness and harmony of the group. Certainly we all enjoyed the sound of the instrument. But we weren't about to let her forget our enjoyment began only after it was installed!

Many times as I lugged it into a service, she heard me tease, "Maude Aimee, why couldn't you have chosen a flute or a French horn? Then you could have carried it yourself!"

"But they that seek the Lord shall not want any good thing." (Psalm 34:10)

CHAPTER 7

From Greenville, we went a short distance northeast to Gastonia, North Carolina, where for two weeks we held our meetings in a Methodist church. From there, our next campaign was slated for Louisville, Kentucky, in the famous old tabernacle of Dr. Mordecai Ham, the man under whose ministry Billy Graham was converted. The Humbard family was particularly honored to get to know Dr. Ham personally, for we always considered it a special blessing to fellowship with other Christians who believed as we did.

This meeting in Louisville turned out to be similar to the old-time meetings which had made the tabernacle famous. Scores of people streamed down the aisles in answer to altar calls. It was apparent people were hungry for the Word of God, told in a simple, unpretentious way, just as the old-time preachers and pioneer evangelists had done years before.

Because Maude Aimee wanted to be near her mother for the birth of our child, we decided she should journey to Dallas while I accompanied the rest of the family to Bowling Green, Kentucky. Naturally, I longed to be with my wife at this time, but I kept busy and tried not to worry about her. It was the first time we had been separated since our marriage, and that made it even worse. She wrote often, saying she was preparing for the baby's arrival and renewing

61

old acquaintances, but between the lines I could detect she felt as I did. Nothing seemed to take the place of our being together. I guess we hadn't realized how slowly time could go by.

A week before the baby's scheduled appearance, I went to Dallas. But no matter how eager we were, the baby seemed in no apparent hurry to be born. Weeks passed. I kept planning for the future, considering the problems of traveling with a small child. It was clear it wasn't going to be quite as easy to pick up and move in the future. Lately I'd noticed it had become more and more difficult for us to find apartments; soon, having a tiny baby with us, we'd find the prospects would not even be as bright as before. All the Humbards had been contemplating the possibility of using house trailers as a solution to the housing problem. Right now it looked as if this might be the ideal solution, even though the initial investment would take a lot of money. We knew God would meet whatever need we had. He always did. I never doubted His promise found in the Book of Matthew, "But seek ye first the kingdom of God, and His righteousness; and all these things shall be added unto you."

One afternoon, Maude Aimee and I set out to look at the house trailers. We hadn't searched long when she discovered a little sixteen-foot one, which contained a living room, bedroom and kitchen—complete with butane heat and cookstove. She loved the trailer at first glance. To most people, it might have seemed not much bigger than a postage stamp, but to us it looked like a home.

I was just figuring out if the price was within the limit we'd set for ourselves and determining the financial arrangements, when Maude Aimee nudged me and announced climatically, "Our house will have to wait for something more important, Rex. I think it's time we start for the hospital."

She tried to calm me as I hurried her to the car and then

raced frantically to Florence Nightingale Hospital. Once there, Maude Aimee was whisked away by the nurses and I was left to pace the floor, each moment expecting to be greeted with the news I'd looked forward to for weeks. But it was a long, long wait. At 5:55 the next morning, I was told I was the father of a chubby, ten-pound boy.

When I saw him, my heart swelled with praise to the Lord. God had given us just what we'd longed for—a healthy boy. He had black curly hair and deep brown eyes. Maude Aimee had prayed her baby would have a cleft chin like his father's, and I guess, as an extra bonus, God granted that and added the hooked nose characteristic of the Humbard family. He was certainly of my image—but I would have loved him, whatever he looked like. He was the son God had entrusted to me! I guess I must have felt a little of what Abraham felt when he looked upon his son. In that moment as I gazed down at him, I prayed God would use this little one for His glory and make him a child—and, eventually, a man—that the Lord would be proud of. I could have no greater desire.

Assured that Maude Aimee was doing well, I returned home to rest after my night's ordeal! Now I resolved my son was going to have his own home and all the comforts which I, with the help of my Heavenly Father, could possibly provide. So, the day Rex, Jr. was born was the day I purchased our first home on wheels. Little did we realize that this little house trailer, and eventually others, a little larger, would be our home for more than ten long years of traveling while we preached the Gospel to everyone who would listen.

Several days after the baby was born, I brought him and his mother back to Maude Aimee's mother's home. I even got to ride in the ambulance with Maude Aimee and hold my son all the way. There was quite a celebration as we arrived—the neighbors gathering around the ambulance, clamoring to see the baby and congratulating us. Finally, we managed to take

Rex, Jr. into the house and lay him in the same bed in which his mother had been born a little over twenty years before. When everything calmed down and Maude Aimee was situated comfortably, I lifted my son in my arms and held him for the rest of the day. I just hated to give the little fellow up. Eventually, however, the nurse insisted, "Please, Reverend Humbard, I have to take care of him when you're gone. I might just as well start now!"

I would relinquish my son only when I had given her specific instructions to be very careful!

The next day, Rex Jr. was five days old. I had to leave Dallas, knowing I wasn't to see him again for over a month. It was necessary that I get back to work, and I kept praying that, with God's help, I'd be able to meet our needs. Though I surely didn't realize it then, God had it all planned in advance.

When I rejoined the evangelistic party, they were on their way to Nashville, Tennessee. Upon arriving, I went to the radio station WSIX to make arrangements for radio time; and, to my surprise, there stood my old friend Jack Woliver, the man who had given us our start in radio at Hot Springs. Now, as program director for WSIX, he gladly scheduled for us two programs a day—free of charge—to help promote our meetings which were being held in Dixie Auditorium in Nashville. He knew us personally, knew we were sincere in the work we were doing, and realized God was blessing us. Obviously he felt no hesitation in giving us what assistance he could along the way.

Three weeks after the broadcasts began, Jack called me into his office and regretfully informed me the management had ordered the programs cancelled, because of lack of available time. The station carrying both the Mutual and the Blue Network broadcasts figured probably there were few listeners for the type of program we were producing.

Both Jack Woliver and I knew differently. People were listening and enjoying the programs, but how could we prove it to the management? Hurriedly, we devised a plan. We printed a postcard bearing the picture of the Humbard family. Then the next day on the broadcasts—both morning and afternoon—we offered it, free and postpaid, to anyone writing to request it. From that one day's announcement, all of us were astounded—the station, Jack Woliver, and the Humbards, too. In the first twelve hours, we received 4,982 pieces of mail. By the end of the day, that number soared to 8,200 requests. We kept both programs.

Because of this encouraging response and the tremendous help of Jack Woliver, we secured, on a sustaining basis, five Mutual Network programs per week, originating from Nashville, Tennessee, and from Bowling Green, Kentucky. Later, when we left Nashville, the network cancelled two of those programs, leaving us only three each week.

A "still, small voice" kept prompting me to do something about the change in schedule, and long ago I had learned to obey God's commands. I had never been to New York City before, but now I felt the Lord was telling me to go there.

Without any specific plans and with very little money, I bought my train ticket and headed for New York. I had learned not to be afraid of circumstances. The only thing I was afraid of was failing to heed God's directions.

"I will instruct thee and teach thee in the way which thou shalt go: I will guide thee with mine eye." (Psalm 32:8)

CHAPTER 8

New York seemed big and noisy and confusing. But still I was determined. Right away I called to make appointments with the Mutual executives and then hurried over to the offices to explain what I wanted—coast-to-coast broadcasts, five days a week.

They turned me down flat, protesting that already there were too many religious broadcasts on Sunday and they certainly didn't want us singing religious songs every day of the week.

"Look, son," they informed me rather condescendingly, "you're lucky to have those three programs a week. Be happy with your luck!"

"It's not luck, sir, and I still want five days a week. I'll offer the programs to someone else."

They laughed. "Go ahead, then. But you'll be back. Those other networks wouldn't even give you three days a week! You'll see."

I walked out of that place and returned to my hotel. New York can seem like the loneliest place in the world. But I shook off discouragement. I knew Someone was with me, guiding me every step of the way. The Lord had led me to New York for a good reason, and it wasn't to be turned down by Mutual Network. With full confidence that I was following God's plan, I left my hotel and went to the NBC Building in Rockefeller Center. There I asked to see the program director of the Blue Network.

"Which one? We have five."

I reached into my briefcase and, to my chagrin, I discovered I didn't have my notes. I'd left them back in the hotel room! Standing there, staring at that receptionist, I couldn't even remember the man's name that Jack Woliver had suggested I see. Quickly I asked for a list of the program directors, thinking I'd recognize the correct name when I saw it. None of the names looked familiar, however, so I just picked the first name on the list.

"Charles Barry. . .I'd like to see Charles Barry, if I may."

Soon I was being ushered down a long carpeted corridor to a door labeled with that name.

"Mr. Barry," I began, "a mutual friend of ours, Jack Woliver of Nashville, Tennessee, told me to come and see you."

Mr. Barry looked at me and grinned. "I don't know Mr. Woliver from Adam, nor you from Eve! Sit down and tell me what you've got on your mind."

It was obvious I was in the wrong office, talking to the wrong man, but there wasn't anything to do but go ahead and try to sell him. I breathed a quick silent prayer and then began to tell Mr. Barry about our program and my desire to have it go out coast-to-coast, five days a week. I soon discovered Mr. Barry had never heard of the Humbards and certainly hadn't heard any of our programs. He asked for a record and I pulled one from my briefcase. Placing it on the turntable, I watched his face as he listened to the Humbard family sing, on our Okeh record release by Columbia Records, a song entitled "Christ Is Keeping My Soul."

Switching the record back to the beginning again, Mr. Barry picked up the receiver of his telephone and asked to speak to his commercial manager.

"Could we sell this?" He played the record through again. Then he put down the phone and turned to me. "What else do you do?" he asked abruptly.

"Well. . .I read poems," I replied.

"What kind?"

I quoted the poem "Flowers."

Mr. Barry stood up behind his desk and announced firmly, "I'll take it! I'll have a hard time selling my boss—he's the man you came here to see—on the idea. If you'd got into his office, he wouldn't even have listened. But I'm going to take it."

I knew then God had guided me right to that very office. I had made a mistake, but it was prompted by the Lord. I thought of that verse, "God works in mysterious ways, his wonders to perform," and I smiled. Everyone quotes that saying, but now I'd seen it proved.

On returning to Nashville, I had a call from New York. It was Charles Barry. We hadn't talked finances at all, only discussing the details of scheduling the programs and deciding to have them shortwaved to the armed services abroad and to Alaska and the ships at sea.

Jack Woliver stood at my elbow, whispering, "Ask him for a sustaining fee."

Without thinking, I did.

Mr. Barry answered, "We can't pay much. We'll have to run telephone lines to get you and we'll have to pay at least three men—a production man, an engineer and an announcer. What would you have to have?"

Questioningly, I turned to Jack Woliver, who was still listening, and he immediately suggested, "Ask him for five hundred a week."

By this time, I felt like the man on the flying trapeze. God hadn't warned me about all this. It was big business. Never before had we been paid anything for a radio program. Getting one on a sustaining basis had been my only hope. But I knew we sure needed money, and if we could get paid for our coast-to-coast broadcasts, it would be manna from heaven.

I said to Charles Barry, "It will inconvenience our meeting some to broadcast from certain points, so I think we should have about $500 a week."

Promptly Mr. Barry replied, "I'll give you $400."

"It's a deal." I instructed, "Send the contract."

I put the phone down. Then I drew a deep breath and tried to still my shaking knees. God had led me through a great experience and had shown me plainly how smoothly everything works out when we follow His plan. The financial burden would now be eased for all of us. The contract was for a year, and the extra money would help us buy what we badly needed—house trailers, cars and equipment.

Excitedly, I rushed out to announce what had happened, stopping only to call long distance to Dallas to tell my wife. It was such a joy—getting to tell the family the good news. But very soon I knew far greater joy when, coast-to-coast, we told a vast radio audience the really Good News of the Gospel of Jesus Christ.

"And they went forth, and preached everywhere, the Lord working with them, and confirming the Word with signs following." (Mark 16:20)

CHAPTER 9

Our new network programs were to begin November 1, 1943, first in Columbus, Ohio, where we were scheduled for meetings. I had to return to Dallas to pick up my wife and son and hitch up the new house trailer. Little Rex, Jr. had already grown more than I could have imagined, and we were eager to stop in Little Rock to show my mother her new grandchild for the first time. Mom was thrilled with our robust little lad, but she kept chuckling about all the black hair he'd been born with—hair hanging almost to his shoulders.

The four of us soon joined the rest of the family and headed north. Once in Columbus, our evening services really capped off very full days; for, each day, before the night meeting, we spent three to five hours in the radio station for rehearsals and actual broadcasts. Rex, Jr.'s presence there didn't hamper us at all. We carried him into the control room, and he'd lie there, not the slightest bit fussy, appearing to thrive on all the noise and excitement. He certainly wasn't aware his life was different from that of other youngsters his age.

After traveling from Columbus to Pittsburgh, Pennsylvania, we held five weeks of meetings in Carnegie Auditorium before moving on to Cincinnati, Ohio. During our five weeks there, we held services in Emery Auditorium. One night the city suffered one of the worst blizzards in its history. Despite that the auditorium which seated 1,800 was filled night after night. We rejoiced that people were so hungry to hear the Gospel, they'd brave terrible snows in order to come.

Our next campaign was in Huntington, West Virginia, and it was there Maude Aimee and I decided to trade our little trailer in for a 25 foot one. The increase in size gave us extra room for a nursery for our growing, active son. Maude Aimee and Rex, Jr. then left for a brief visit to Dallas while I went on to Akron, Ohio, for services held in Central High School Auditorium and broadcasts originating from WAKR. My family rejoined me, shortly, to share the good fellowship of wonderful Christian people in Akron and to see the tremendous encouragement from the Lord in those meetings. I felt a strange warmth for these people who eagerly listened to every word of the Gospel message and then went out, determined to let God's presence show in their lives.

For some time I had been vexed with tire trouble. It was easy in those times to grumble about tires or gasoline rationing, particularly because we were on the move almost constantly. Fortunately, I finally managed to locate a tire at the cost of $50. But the next one was priced at $60 and lasted only fifteen miles. I was pretty disgusted and hunted around until I found a third tire and tube for $90. Forty miles was the most I managed to wring from that one before it blew out. After our next meetings in Cleveland, Ohio, and Erie, Pennsylvania, we had still more tire trouble. I searched frantically to find a tire for the trailer at the bargain price of $50, for by this time my financial situation was desperate. I'd even been forced to dig into tithe money to keep tires on the car and trailer.

Just a few miles outside of Erie, my newest tire blew. I got out. All was quiet, and eventually Maude Aimee turned around to check on what the delay could be. She was shocked to see me kneeling on that busy highway, oblivious to the stares of amazed motorists passing by. I was praying, "Oh, God, I'm sorry. I'll pay my tithes. . .I promise I'll pay my tithes!"

There was nothing to do but park the trailer there by the side of the road and leave it until we could find tires. Despite the fact the trailer door had a faulty lock and the trailer remained there three full days, everything was safe when we returned. We had left it in God's hands, and He watched over it.

In the days that followed, I got caught up on my tithe money, and from then on we had no more serious tire problems. It was a lesson I'll never forget. When I preached on tithing from that day forward, I preached from experience. I saw how disastrous it could be to hold back from God the part that belongs to Him. The Lord had clearly shown me that if a person gives the Lord His due, the rest of his money will be sufficient for all his needs.

Other trials had focused on us, previous to this, in Erie, Pennsylvania. During one of the services a big storm tore the tent badly. Water poured through the holes until the ground inside the tent was covered. We tried to dismiss the meeting and send the people home, but they refused to go. They huddled under their umbrellas with their feet held off the ground and let the rain pour in. It was apparent God was there, pouring down blessings right along with the rain.

We journeyed to Battle Creek, Michigan, to hold our next meeting in a large auditorium which had never before been the scene of religious services. Huge crowds assembled nightly, and God made it a great revival. Also in Battle Creek, the Percy Jones Hospital was filled with servicemen who had returned with serious injuries. We held services in every room—preaching, singing and praying with the men. It was an answer to our prayers—a God-given opportunity to expand our ministry to the armed forces, beyond our regularly scheduled broadcasts that were being shortwaved to the troops overseas. We praised God for this privilege of meeting them personally, and we continued to work in these hospital visits just as often as our busy schedule allowed.

Next we went on to a meeting in Jackson, Michigan, for just nine days. The weather was so bad it was a hardship to live in the trailers. Snow was piled high, often mounting in drifts to where we barely could open our trailer doors. After much prayer, we came to the decision it would be best to head south. We knew it would be tremendously difficult to secure enough gasoline under the strict rationing regulations, but God miraculously worked out the arrangements. He was leading us to the destination where He could use us best. We left Michigan, bound for Oklahoma, stopping on the way at Hot Springs for Christmas. Finally we reached Tulsa and began our third great meeting in Convention Hall.

Our first year's time on the networks was almost up. It had been a great year. God had taken care of us and seen us through all our financial difficulties. He had enlarged our field of witness and brought hundreds of souls to Himself. All the Humbards kept praising the Lord, for we could testify that God constantly does "exceeding abundantly above all that we ask or think."

"The steps of a good man are ordered by the Lord: and he delighteth in his way." (Psalm 37:23)

CHAPTER 10

I was searching for an answer to a major problem—how to advance our future meetings more effectively and, at the same time, complete the details involved in the current meetings. If I traveled ahead and took care of all the advance work for the next meeting—advertising, radio programs, city permits, rentals, ushers and personal workers, I couldn't be on hand to close the present meeting. More and more we realized that doing a good job for the Lord depended on planning details carefully in advance. Attendance was growing, responsibilities increasing. The problem had to be solved.

As with other problems, I took the matter to the Lord. And as with other problems, I had the assurance the Lord already was bringing about His plan. I knew when it came, it would be the best possible answer. Throughout the years I'd found the joy of the words from the Book of Isaiah, "before they call, I will answer; and while they are yet speaking, I will hear."

Back in Hot Springs that Christmas season one of our childhood friends, Wayne Jones, had been gloriously saved. Even prior to this experience, Wayne's life had been closely linked to ours. Personable, fun-loving, Wayne was brought up under the sound of our ministry. But he had never made a definite decision to claim Jesus Christ as his Saviour. He had gone to school with us and had been courting my sister Leona for a long time. Frequently we'd see him hanging around, and we'd tease him about his devotion to "The Little Lamb," our nickname for gentle Leona.

Wayne loved flying and intended making it his career. He became a flight instructor at Muskogee, Oklahoma, and was doing extremely well, rapidly advancing in his chosen field. Gradually he got away from his early home training and the influence of a wonderful Christian mother, and he continued to resist the efforts of a church which constantly prayed for his soul. He began drinking and living like the other men with whom he worked.

That year, 1944, we had returned to Hot Springs for the holidays and Wayne happened to come home, too. Still in love with Leona, he was drawn immediately to the services at church, for it seemed the only way possible to be able to see his girl. She didn't let anything interfere with serving the Lord. At church that night God gripped his heart. Wayne felt the burden of his sin, and in one shattering moment he knew he had to turn to God. Kneeling at the altar, he found his way to the Saviour and arose a radiant child of God.

That very day when his heart was changed, Wayne felt the call to the Lord's service. He could hardly believe what was happening to him. He walked around in a daze, muttering to himself, "How can God use someone like me?"

But he had no doubt God had intervened. Not only had the Lord ransomed his soul, He had claimed his life!

Early that January before we left Hot Springs, Wayne and Leona had become engaged. He returned to his base of operations in Muskogee, but this time things were different. When he was asked to fly over to Arkansas to bring back a case of liquor for one of their parties, Wayne staunchly refused.

"You fellows will have to get someone else to do that stuff now. I was saved when I went home for Christmas, and now I'm going to live right."

The other officers were stunned, but no amount of teasing or pleading altered Wayne's position. It wasn't long before their ridicule turned to respect.

When we went to Tulsa, Oklahoma, for our next meeting, Wayne flew up each night to join us for the service. Distance was nothing to a pilot, and Wayne was drawn to Tulsa as effectively as a moth is drawn to a flame. Previously, Leona's presence had been the reason for his flashing smile in the front row, but it wasn't the whole cause now. Wayne was seeking more of God. He discovered he was hungry to know God's Word, to grow in wisdom and understanding of the Gospel he'd neglected for so many years. Wayne gave his testimony frequently in those meetings, and everyone was thrilled at the change in his life.

During his visits, whenever there was time, Wayne took us flying. Often before—from a safe vantage point on the ground—I had watched him perform breathtaking tricks in the air. Now I asked him to try a few spins with me in the plane. He was delighted to comply. I saw him smile broadly as he went into a series of twists. There was no mistake as to what Wayne had in store for me! As soon as the wild demonstration was ended, Wayne glanced back to see how I was taking it. I wasn't in my seat. I was under it.

Despite that initiation, the matter of flying began to interest me. I kept wondering if this was part of the answer to that prayer I'd prayed, months before, about advance arrangements for our meetings.

After we closed the Tulsa campaign, we moved to Muskogee for nightly services. Since our network programs were finished, we were a little less pressed for time. Coupled with this advantage, Wayne was still stationed in Muskogee and volunteered as an enthusiastic flight instructor. It wasn't long before we had all flown enough to feel at home in a plane, and I had completed my training and received a pilot's license.

The next step was to secure a plane. It was obvious it would cost a lot more money than we had right then, but God had an answer to that problem, too. The government was selling off surplus planes at Muskogee, and Wayne's company serviced these planes to prepare them for licensing. I asked Wayne about the possibility of purchasing one of them. Before we left Muskogee in March, 1945, the transaction was completed. We now had our own plane.

Following services in Fort Smith, we held a great meeting in our home church, the Gospel Temple in Hot Springs. There, before we left in June, 1945, Leona and Wayne were married in a quiet, but moving ceremony performed by Reverend John Hendricks. Although none of us suspected it then, he was later to become attached to the Humbard family himself, for eventually he and Wayne's widowed mother were to be married. God's steps are sure and right. . .and are accomplished in the fullness of His time. We have only to watch and follow, to find the Lord's best for our lives.

My now-radiant little sister Leona returned with her bridegroom to Muskogee to begin their new life together. The rest of us went on to Houston, Texas, for our next meeting. It attracted enormous crowds and was blessed so abundantly by God that it was held over for six weeks. But the absence of Wayne and Leona left us all a little dissatisfied. Something seemed wrong. None of us said much, but we all felt it.

After two weeks, I called Wayne and invited them to join our party, to travel with us permanently. Wayne hesitated a moment before replying and then said, "Rex, I'd like to, but what could I do? How could I be of use to you and the Lord?"

I was encouraged by his immediate question about serving the Lord. Since I believed this was part of God's answer to my prayer for guidance, I explained, "Well, you can do the flying, and other things will open up. I feel God has a use for both of you here. He'll show us what He wants."

Our conversation left me optimistic—certain that God was moving. And yet, for Wayne, the actual decision was still to be made, and it was a difficult one. It appeared God was reminding him of the call to service he'd received when he'd been converted—a call he had never fully understood. He had not discussed it with anyone else. But suddenly he was sure God was working out the plan for his life.

To join an evangelistic party involved a big financial sacrifice for them. Understanding this, when his boss learned Wayne was contemplating leaving, he offered Wayne more money. His company had no intentions of losing such a good man. Wayne and Leona discussed it thoroughly again. They prayed, and God showed them this change was His will. Having made their final decision, they prepared to join us as soon as possible. Wayne and Leona didn't want to take the slightest chance of disobeying God.

Our great meeting in Houston finally closed, and from there we had no immediately pressing engagement. We all were tired and in need of a change. Clement and his new bride, Priscilla, seemed grateful that a short break in the schedule would make it possible for them to take a honeymoon. Leona and Wayne also anticipated getting off by themselves for a trip and, of course, Maude Aimee and I had never had a real wedding trip, either. This seemed to be the golden opportunity for all of us. Excitedly we made our plans for separate little vacations, carefully avoiding mention of destination to the others.

Maude Aimee and I had always wanted to see Mexico City. But now with the opportunity to go, my wife was torn between two desires. She didn't want to be separated from our eighteen-month old son but still knew it wouldn't be practical to take a toddler to Mexico. I knew how desperately she wanted to make the trip, so I left the decision to her. She finally reached the conclusion that Rex, Jr. would be in good hands if her mother came to Houston to take care of him. Maude Aimee's enthusiasm waned, however, when the moment of departure actually arrived.

When we boarded the airplane, Maude Aimee was tear-stained. We settled in our seats, and she waved to little Rex, standing beside his grandmother. But as the plane moved down the field, her tears returned, noisily. Passengers glared at me. I realized they thought I was the cause of her heartbreak, and I tried to comfort her. Nothing I said seemed to help. I gave up and started praying. Through that cloud of tears, Maude Aimee began to notice the attitudes of the people around her, and I guess her conscience was pricked. For my sake, she perked up. By the time we'd landed on the outskirts of Mexico City, she was her usual exuberant self.

The startling contrasts of this cosmopolitan city struck us forcibly. Exotic scenery and beautiful buildings in the heart of the city only heightened the tragedy of the appalling poverty in the slums. As I looked at them, my heart felt burdened for the empty hearts and souls which lodged there.

We had reservations at the lovely Lincoln Hotel, which had been open only a month. I was busy registering when I heard Maude Aimee's amazed cry. She had just spied Clement and Priscilla, who had had no idea we'd be anywhere near. As we were laughing about it, we noticed other familiar faces. Reverend and Mrs. Albert Ott, of Maude Aimee's church in Dallas, walked down the hall. We were delighted to learn they were assigned to a room two doors away from ours. All of us had a grand time on that vacation, although we tried to give the newlyweds—Clement and Priscilla—as much privacy as possible. Certainly we understood their desire to be alone.

Maude Aimee was ecstatic when we took the boat ride, serenaded by gondoliers. She marveled at the profusion of brilliant flowers throughout the city and became even more excited when I took her to see her first opera. It was worth the whole trip to know I'd made her happy. I thought she bore up admirably under the strain of separation from Rex, Jr. A few days later, however, as we returned to Houston, Maude Aimee could barely wait for the miles to pass to get back to her boy.

Out on the road again bound for Memphis, we were content to be back in the Lord's work. The rest had restored our vitality. Once we arrived in Memphis, we began preparing enthusiastically for the four-week meeting in City Auditorium. Following this, I decided to fly our own plane to Nashville, Tennessee, to do the advance work for our next meeting.

On the night I was supposed to return to Memphis, I was flying southwest, approaching the Tennessee Valley, when I ran into a storm. Visibility was so low I was forced to turn back, altering my course to take me up into Kentucky around the edge of the storm and then back into Tennessee. By the time I had completed the maneuver, it was getting dark. I had no radio and no night lights. I didn't even have the vaguest idea of my location. All alone, high above the earth, I had only God to depend on. I kept flying south, praying every moment for guidance.

Suddenly, I saw a small red flashing light. I smiled for the first time in what seemed like ages. To me, it was God's flashlight. Turning the nose of the plane toward that tiny beacon, I flew straight at it. But before I could arrive at the source of the light, complete darkness had fallen. I'll never know just how I missed the high tension wires or how I made the final approach to a field without landing lights, but, somehow, I managed to land.

I alighted from the plane, mighty thankful for that solid ground beneath me. Looking around as much as I could in that darkness, I noticed I'd landed on what appeared to be an auxiliary field for commercial airlines. Approaching a tiny building at the corner of the field, I found a lone man on duty. He informed me this was a cross-point for several routes.

"I don't have a car here," he apologized, "so there's no transportation to get you into town until the relief man shows up around midnight. You're welcome to wait here."

"What's the nearest town?" I asked.

"Just a small place—Henderson, Tennessee," was his answer.

When I eventually got there, I discovered Henderson had no hotel. I made a few inquiries and finally managed to rent a room in a private home. Then I tried to call Memphis. The phone was dead. The storm had damaged the lines and service was completely cut off.

As I waited for the weather to clear and dawn to come, I kept thinking how I would have been lost without God's guidance. I thought about the many times in life when all of us run into storms so severe we get off the right track. We miss the pathway we're supposed to follow. And yet God is always there. Jesus said, "I am the light of the world." He is the ray of light in our darkness. He is always there waiting, always shining, always accessible if we'll look to Him.

I pondered the love of God for me and for all men, and I got down on my knees to praise the Lord for His deliverance. I could have crashed the plane and been lost in those mountains, never to return. Then I thought how, years before, He'd offered me another "airfield of mercy." In my sin and darkness, I had seen the beacon of Jesus Christ. I had found the only way to safety and security man can ever know.

If I could live a million years, I knew I could never praise the Lord enough.

"For our light affliction, which is but for a moment, worketh for us a far more exceeding and eternal weight of glory." (II Corinthians 4:17)

CHAPTER 11

Daytona Beach, Florida, was the scene of our next meeting. We opened Sunday afternoon for a great service. The blessing was repeated again in the service that night.

At dawn Monday, we were wakened by loud pounding on our trailer door. Sleepily, I stumbled to open it. Two tall policemen confronted me. I stared in surprise as they began to speak. "Are you the Humbards?"

"Yes," I replied, more than a trifle confused.

"Well, the City Auditorium has just burned. . .almost to the ground. We managed to save the tractor next to the building, but we couldn't get to the trailer. Everything inside the building is gone, too."

He saw my face, and as he turned away, I heard his voice soften, "Sorry, mister, hope you didn't lose much."

It was a staggering blow. The trailer and the musical equipment within the building had been worth more than $14,000. None of it was covered by insurance. We drove out to view the disaster. With sinking hearts, we saw the smoking ruins. All the instruments so necessary to our ministry—instruments we'd collected for fourteen years—were gone.

Turning to our bewildered little group, I said, "Well, here's where we use the faith we preach. You know what we tell folks when trouble comes: 'All things work together for good to them that love God, to them who are the called according to His purpose.' If we quote that verse from Romans to others, we've got to believe it ourselves."

As I talked to them, I knew I was speaking to myself, as well. I was renewing my own trust in the Lord. Trying to stand a little straighter, I encouraged, "All right now, let's get busy."

That's exactly what we did. We had announced revival services. . .and revival services were what we were going to have. Fire or no fire!

By the time our radio program went on the air that afternoon, we already had secured the necessary permissions to use the high school auditorium. I mentioned on our broadcast the meeting would open that night, as previously announced. For the radio program that day, we had sung without any instruments, so I added that we'd be grateful if anyone in the audience who had any musical instruments would loan them to us for a few days until we could start replacing ours.

If we trust God at His Word, He works everyhing out to His glory, even in a calamity such as this. When the public heard our services were going on despite our loss, crowds poured into the meeting. Many who, otherwise, would never have entered a revival meeting, now visited out of curiosity. They could see we practiced what we preached. And once they heard God's Word proclaimed, they found they were hungry to know the loving Saviour, who could carry His children through trials victoriously.

That first Monday night three instruments arrived on loan for the musical portion of the program—a guitar, a mandolin and a solovox. The Spirit of the Lord was evident in the service. We played and sang as we never had before. We were anything but defeated. What was money measured against the worth of a soul!

For three nights we held meetings in the high school auditorium, with scores of people coming to the altar each service. Then a local man suggested we might like to use a tent he owned. Someone else loaned us plush seats from an auditorium in town. We erected the tent on the ball field and began tent meetings.

Then, hardship struck again. During the early morning hours following our second service in the tent, one of Florida's vicious tropical storms smashed across Daytona Beach. Daylight came, and we rushed out to find the tent torn to shreds and the attractive plush seats ruined.

Still undaunted, we moved back into the high school and went right on with our meetings. By this time, almost everyone in town and people in the surrounding areas had heard of our misfortunes. The crowds doubled. Before the meetings closed, we saw hundreds of lives changed by their surrender to Jesus Christ.

Moving on to Miami, we discovered the story of our loss had preceded us. People were curious. The news stories attracted hundreds who would never have thought of attending under less publicized circumstances. We felt the blessing of God in a most unusual way. Again we started buying instruments, replacing one at a time. We knew the Lord would help us and He did. Our equipment was on the way to being restored. Souls had been saved in abundance. Our hearts were so full with the blessing of God that we echoed again: "For we know that all things work together for good to them that love God, to them who are the called according to His purpose."

Once again, Dallas became our stopping-off point. While we held services in Bethel Temple, we made preparations for our first West Coast tour. The previous war years had made such a trip impossible, primarily because of gasoline restrictions. But now we felt God was calling us to go there.

We decided to sell our plane before we left. It had served us well, but right now we could use the money it would bring more than the plane itself. After assembling all we'd need for many months, we started off. Traveling west, we planned to visit some of God's majestic scenes along the way—Carlsbad Caverns, the Grand Canyon, all the beauties of nature that constantly reminded us of God's words: "Eye hath not seen, nor ear heard, neither have entered into the heart of man, the things which God hath prepared for them that love Him." In comparison to this earthly magnificence, think of what God has in store for us in heaven!

The first meeting on the West Coast was scheduled for Angeles Temple in Los Angeles. That building, seating more than 5,500, was packed to capacity. There wasn't even standing room. We were delighted that our southern style music was going to be popular here on the California coast. Already the appeal was obvious. If we could attract people to the meetings, we knew God was able to speak to them. He alone could convict their hearts and lead them to salvation.

Los Angeles also became the place we made our first four recordings for Sacred Records. We were extremely busy there with our radio programs, plus the main feature of our days—the nightly service.

Lovely San Gabriel was our next stop. We considered it a privilege to have as the location of our services the playhouse within the Old San Gabriel Mission. And, night after night, one visitor surprised us. Holding a prominent seat in our audience was a priest, who seemed to have the time of his life singing along with the crowd. Our type of program was something new to the residents of this town. They responded enthusiastically. We saw God's blessings abundantly outpoured.

Midway through the meetings a politician from that area stopped by to request the use of the auditorium for one night. He planned to confront a young lawyer in a debate on current political issues.

"I realize you have the rental for a full 30 days," he explained, "but would you mind letting us use it for one night?"

"You can have it if you pay the rent for that night," I stipulated, "but there's just one condition. The Humbards will come to the debate, announce our meetings and then play some music for about 20 minutes before the debate starts."

This seemed to me to be a great opportunity for reaching people not usually exposed to church services.

The California politician readily assented. The debate was scheduled, and the night arrived. We played and sang our Gospel songs for a short time before we made the announcement about our future services and then followed that with more music. Then the two debaters were introduced—the political incumbent who had interviewed me earlier about the auditorium, and his opponent, a rising young lawyer running for Congress named Richard M. Nixon. Before the meeting was over, the handsome, youthful Nixon had thoroughly trounced his opponent.

In the future I was to become interested to see the young debater go on to win that Congressional election and go to the nation's Capitol. Years later, on a trip to Washington, I encountered the Vice President during the Eisenhower administration. It was, of course, Richard Nixon. As we were introduced, I smiled and inquired, "Do you happen to remember participating in a debate at San Gabriel Playhouse years ago?"

Mr. Nixon's eyes twinkled brightly as he ushered us into his office. "Yes, and I couldn't possibly forget all those banjos and bottles and bells the Humbard family played!"

When Mr. Nixon himself took the oath of office as President of the United States on that crisp January morning in 1969, I couldn't help recalling how, years before, I'd presented, in song, the wonderful news of Jesus Christ at one of his first political rallies.

Long Beach, Riverside, San Bernardino and Fresno were all scenes of great meetings in those months on the Coast. The time flew by swiftly as we witnessed God moving in the hearts and lives of people there.

The weather was sunny and mild. Every bright morning we regretted not bringing along a tent for our western tour. This was just the place for a tent. I finally went out and purchased a portable B-29 plane hangar, and we hauled it up to Bakersfield. There the tent caused considerable comment, for it was a peculiar looking thing.

When we were erecting it, a man strolled over and asked, "What are you putting up—another Golden Gate Bridge?"

I chuckled. "No, a Gospel tent."

The man laughed heartily. "You could get all the Christians in this town into the first two rows of seats in that place."

"That's fine," I countered. "Then this is just the place for us. That's what we're looking for—non-Christians who will listen to the Word of God."

The first night the place was packed. Cars were parked everywhere. A State Highway Patrolman came in, complaining that cars were blocking the highway. Midway through the song service, I asked everyone to cooperate by moving their cars in order to clear the roads. The patrolman stayed a few more moments to listen and then moved out to the road, only to return in a very short time. People had moved the cars as he'd instructed, but, in doing so, they'd blocked him in. In good humor, he sat down and stayed to enjoy the rest of the service with them.

Bakersfield could be described in terms the Bible uses—"ripe unto harvest." When we left there, we felt many more hearts were trusting in the Saviour than when we'd first arrived.

We moved on to Pasadena and then back to Angeles Temple for a four-week revival service which drew gigantic crowds. Two days after the conclusion of that meeting, on August 5, Maude Aimee was admitted to Queen of Angels Hospital, and we welcomed a nine-pound, ten-ounce baby boy into our family. We named him Don Raymond. His sunny disposition was apparent right from the very beginning. When he was three days old, I brought him and his mother back to the trailer and took on the jobs of nursemaid, cook and bottlewasher. My early training in helping raise one brother and four sisters certainly came in mighty handy.

When Donnie—as we dubbed him—was nine days old, he began traveling with us, getting initiated early to what would be normal routine for the next six years. We set up the tent in Pomona, California, and began services. Less than two weeks after the baby was born, Maude Aimee joined us on the platform, singing once again. But evidently it was too early for her to resume strenuous activity. She contracted a bad cold, becoming so ill the doctors insisted she be taken back to Los Angeles to be treated by the physician who had delivered the baby. Thankful for an invitation to a friend's home there, she recuperated for two weeks. Meanwhile, I managed to drive up every day to help her as much as I could with the baby.

We were now planning a series of meetings in the Northwest. When my wife had recovered from her illness and Don was four weeks old, we left for Portland, Oregon. But, on the way, another testing from the Lord occurred. Dad Humbard was badly injured in a serious automobile accident.

Hospitalized with a fractured hip, he was advised by the doctors he would be confined for a long time. They gave us very little encouragement he'd ever walk again.

We didn't give up hope, even for one second. We knew the Great Physician. Daily we held to God's promises, confidently expecting Dad Humbard, not only to recover from pain, but to walk again, erect as ever. With God, nothing is impossible.

"I will go before thee, and make the crooked places straight." (Isaiah 45:2)

CHAPTER 12

Sudden readjustments had to be made. The Portland meeting was scheduled to open immediately. Dad was in the hospital and Mom felt compelled to stay with him, as the doctors declared he shouldn't be left alone. Previously, Clement and I each had rarely preached more than one service per week. Wayne, too, spoke occasionally. But Mother and Dad were really the backbone of the preaching ministry.

We prayed about it, knowing the meetings must go on despite their absence. I rested my complete dependence on the guidance of the Lord. Only with His help could we assume full responsibility and handle the meetings successfully. The duties attached to a big campaign were numerous. And one of the greatest difficulties was there was only limited time to study. God had given us a tremendous test. I started seeking God as never before, and I found myself plunged into a great experience with the Lord.

Considering the circumstances, humanly speaking, the Portland meetings could easily have turned into a fiasco. Dad was suffering. The doctors held out little hope. We found out even preachers can grow discouraged.

But God's work doesn't follow "human" patterns. The meetings began to glow with the presence of God. We had sought a closer walk with Him. We'd thrown ourselves completely over to His guidance and help. God met our need as He always had. The sermons touched hearts. Many people turned to Jesus Christ. We saw men and women, boys and girls repenting of their sin, weeping at the altar. Others brought to God, in prayer, their troubled minds and bodies, and we saw God heal. That Portland meeting gave us new faith. We couldn't deny the fact that all strength rests in the Lord. He had used us in misfortune to bring glory to Himself.

It was at this time, when we were praising God together, that for the first time Wayne felt impelled to reveal to me God had definitely called him to a life of full-time Christian service.

"I've never understood it," he marveled, "but I know what I'm called to do. God spoke to my heart and called me to be an assistant pastor to some great man of God. The Lord told me the very day He saved me. If it hadn't been for that, I'd probably never have joined this evangelistic party." Then, musing softly, he added, "You know, there must be a great need for men to serve as assistants. Surely God needs men to assist just as much as He needs true men of God to lead."

Wayne had no idea right then where God would place him, or why God impressed him to open his heart to me and disclose his secret. But my heart was warmed by his devotion to God's work. His simple faith, his determination to seek God's will and not his own ambition was sure to be rewarded.

Had we stopped to analyze our experiences in those busy days, undoubtedly we would have seen God was preparing us to be used in a greater way. This was only His workshop for us. Already I had experienced a ministry of music, a thorough exposure to business details, a training in touching the public as a master-of-ceremonies, and, finally, the wonderful joy of preaching God's Word. But the Lord had more in store for me. Step by step, He led forward toward future plans.

We closed that victorious meeting in Portland and drove to Seattle, opening in a church full of Swedish and Norwegian people. They'd grown used to an entirely different style of music and preaching. We prayed about this matter and felt God meant us to stick to our own individual southern style. It turned out to be a happy choice, for the very novelty of it intrigued those Scandinavians. The meeting became one of the most remarkable in the history of our campaigns.

Many individuals who for years had belonged to this church had never known the true joy of salvation in Jesus Christ. People at every service, hungry for a personal relationship with God, made their way to the altar to seek His salvation. The first woman who came forward testified she'd never before heard of "being born again." Once she herself found salvation through Christ, she couldn't rest until she had convinced everyone she knew that he also needed this marvelous spiritual rebirth. The church was packed every night. All standing room was taken. Eventually we even had to turn people away because of lack of space.

Throughout the Northwest the meetings continued. From Seattle, we moved to Olympia, the state capitol of Washington, and then on to California for a one-week meeting in a high school. We kept as close to Dad as possible. Constantly we prayed for his recovery, and soon it became apparent our prayers were being answered. Dad had improved so noticeably that we felt it safe to leave the area, entrusting him fully to Mom's devoted care. We moved south, taking meetings down into California once again.

At the time of our sixth wedding anniversary, Maude Aimee and I were in Stockton, California, midway through a tent meeting. It seemed possible for us to take two days off to visit the interesting sights of San Francisco, as part of our family celebration. On our way there we passed through

Oakland. I noticed a brand new church building which so attracted me I stopped to read the bulletin board on the church lawn. Oakland's Neighborhood Church appeared to me to be the most beautiful church I'd ever seen.

Jokingly, I remarked, "Wouldn't it be great to go in there and hold one of our old-fashioned revival meetings? I'd love to preach the old-time religion in that spectacular, modern setting!"

We went on our way, and after we'd closed the Stockton meeting, we traveled to Lodi, a community of 10,000 people, most of whom were in the vineyard business. It was estimated that every night there were over 5,000 in attendance. That was quite a record for a town that size.

One afternoon while we were in Lodi, a couple of men walked up and introduced themselves.

"I'm Earl Sexauer, and this is my musical director," the smiling gentleman began as he pointed to the man beside him. "Here's my card. We heard the Humbard family back in 1944, in Cleveland, Ohio. The Christian and Missionary Alliance National Conference was being held in the Euclid Avenue Baptist Church, that big old structure built by John D. Rockefeller. Remember the place? You people played and sang for the convention, and right then I said to myself, 'Someday, Earl, when we build our new church, it would be wonderful to have that family for our opening services!' Boy, I certainly didn't dream then that all the prayers for a new church would be answered this soon, and we'd happen to come together here. Rex, would you hold a meeting in our church right away?"

In amazement I read the card handed to me. It said, "Oakland's Neighborhood Church, the cathedral of tomorrow."

That was the church which had only recently been completed and had caused such a stir all over the West Coast.

Now they were asking us to take part in their opening! As we talked, I discovered these men of God preached the very same "old-time religion" that we did.

It wasn't hard to make up my mind. "We'd like nothing better than to join you for the opening, Reverend Sexauer," I agreed enthusiastically.

I could hardly wait to see the inside of the magnificent structure. I wasn't disappointed, either. The meeting itself was one of our greatest revival meetings. As many as 200 people went to the altar in one night. The building was crowded for each service, and night after night God touched hearts and lives for His glory.

The church's famous Port-O'-Call attracted many servicemen in the Bay Area. We were thrilled to participate in the meetings for them, also. Earl Sexauer was famous on the West Coast for his illustrated sermons, and the unusual features of his auditorium were designed to enhance that ministry. This method was a favorite of mine, as well, but tent meetings are not easily adapted to the use of visual aids. One evening when it was announced we would play the 28 cow bells, we were astonished to see the choir being lifted into the air by a hydraulic lift, and another stage appearing, on which cowbells and sleighbells were suspended artistically. Earl's ideas topped everything!

The friendship between Earl and me deepened. We never tired of telling of the blessing of God in our lives. We shared experiences and participated in daily radio programs originating in his church. Then we joined in services connected with the Bay Area Youth for Christ. It was a busy, happy time.

After two weeks of services in Fresno, California—our last California meeting, we got the splendid news that Dad had recuperated sufficiently to journey back to Arkansas. With thankful hearts, we started home.

Our fourth great meeting in Convention Hall in Tulsa, Oklahoma, was followed by a meeting in Barlesville, Oklahoma, in a local high school. The heat was so oppressive, however, that the audience couldn't stand it. We closed the meeting after only a week. Next we tried Coffeyville, Kansas, but the heat wave had followed us there, and again it became necessary to close the meeting early.

In Pittsburg, Kansas, the home of Kansas State College, we held an open air meeting. Although the weather was still hot, the meetings were pleasant out in the open and attendance remained high for our three weeks there. Our next stop was Kansas City, and from there we traveled to South Bend, Indiana, to hold a revival in the South Bend Tabernacle, Lester Sumrall's church. We were pushing for an increase for his Sunday School, and a wonderful meeting resulted. The church broke all Sunday School records.

Bond Bowman's Assembly of God church in Detroit invited us next, and it was there we first heard the catchy little chorus "Everybody Ought To Know" and decided to use it temporarily as a theme song.

A return to Cadle Tabernacle in Indianapolis, Indiana, for a series of services had been eagerly anticipated. This had been the scene of our wedding, and the fond memories of the city and our friends there remained with us vividly. But the visit was not to be the joyful one we expected.

For some time we'd noticed that Rex, Jr. had been coughing. He had gone swimming in Lake Michigan recently, and it was easy to excuse the symptoms as those of a stubborn summer cold. Rex, Jr. had always been such a healthy child, with no serious infections, and the cough seemed relatively easy to explain.

But the illness hung on. His mother and I grew increasingly concerned as he at times encountered difficulty in breathing. Many nights we were up with him, trying in vain to soothe the persistent cough.

Finally, we took him to a doctor, and after performing a careful examination, the physician gravely gave us his news. Rex, Jr.'s left lung was so affected that two-thirds of it had collapsed. He was in an advanced stage of tuberculosis. Young Rex must be put to bed immediately, treated with penicillin, and given constant care and medication every two hours, day and night. Suddenly it seemed as if the bottom had dropped out of our world.

"And ye shall seek me, and find me, when ye shall search for me with all your heart." (Jeremiah 29:13)

CHAPTER 13

Rex, Jr.'s life was in the hands of God. All our lives we'd depended on the Lord of hosts as our Sustainer. To turn to prayer for this longing of our hearts now was to turn to the only source of help we'd ever known. We had seen God accomplish many miracles, for to be in God's work is to observe a constant miracle. To see the transformation of a sinful, hopeless soul into a redeemed, radiant child of God, through faith in Jesus Christ, is to witness the greatest example of the supernatural. Every day we were faced with the fact that God can do what no man could ever do.

Once in a while, however, when it comes to praying for someone as close to us as one's own child, there is an element of fear that enters in. When it means so much to us personally, we find our faith needs a boost. Though we sought the Lord with all our hearts, still Rex, Jr. didn't improve.

Maude Aimee called her brother in Fort Worth, Texas, and after revealing how serious Rex, Jr.'s condition was, requested that he too pray for our son.

"Why don't you get in touch with Oral Roberts?" was his reply.

My wife was puzzled, but eager to go anywhere, do anything, if God wanted us to do so.

"Who is Oral Roberts?" she asked.

Her brother explained this minister from Tulsa, Oklahoma, had himself been afflicted with tuberculosis in his youth. His heart was particularly burdened for those with similar affliction. He tried to share his own faith with others, encouraging them that God could heal.

I found Maude Aimee strongly urging me to take Rex, Jr. to one of Oral Roberts' meetings. After investigating, we learned he was next scheduled for a service in Mobile, Alabama. But when she consulted the doctor about the wisdom of taking the child that far, he advised against it and suggested Rex, Jr. be placed in a sanitarium. Maude Aimee and I couldn't even consider that solution. We strongly believed God could heal our child, for He had given us—as His children—the Scriptural command found in the book of James, "Is any sick among you? let him call for the elders of the church; and let them pray over him, anointing him with oil in the name of the Lord: and the prayer of faith shall save the sick, and the Lord shall raise him up . . . "

The doctor finally consented to allow Rex, Jr. to go, if we would take care to make it a leisurely trip, so as not to tire him. There was sufficient time before the meeting in Mobile for us to proceed slowly, stopping along the way to allow our son all the rest he needed.

Arriving in the southern city, we made our way to the tent service, going early because of the large crowds. We responded to the invitation for those who wanted prayer to come forward. The evangelist had been notified by Maude Aimee's brother, Charles Jones, of our coming. He prayed fervently for Maude Aimee and me, asking God to bless us as servants in the Lord's work, that our lives would continue to be dedicated to preaching the Gospel. Then placing a hand on Rex, Jr., he asked the Lord to heal him of the tuberculosis which had attacked him.

Raising his head at the end of the simple prayer, he turned to us and said, "Go now and don't worry. The Lord has done the job."

We accepted the answer in faith and left rejoicing, thinking of the words God spoke to Jeremiah, "Behold, I am the Lord, the God of all flesh; is there anything too hard for me?"

In the services that followed, we took advantage of the opportunity to "take in" instead of "giving out" continually, as we were in the habit of doing. Hearing God's Word brings refreshment to the mind and soul. Sometimes even preachers grow weary when troubles pile up. This period of time given to hearing the Gospel message and meditating on His blessings to us as His children brought comfort to our hearts. Then we went to Miami for services. Already we felt invigorated.

Rex, Jr. had stopped coughing immediately, and he appeared to improve right before our eyes. How grateful we were for God's mercy. Not only had He healed our son, but He had stimulated our faith and renewed our desire to bring glory to Him. Four weeks after Rex, Jr. was prayed for, we took him to a specialist who examined him thoroughly. The doctor pronounced him in perfect health. Then we showed the physician the former x-rays which pictured his lungs in an advanced stage of tuberculosis. Amazed, the doctor immediately ordered additional x-rays to be taken, plus a complete fluoroscopic examination of the child. We knew Rex, Jr. was well, but we wanted proof so our testimony would be complete.

When the results were ready, the doctor repeated that the pictures showed the child's lungs were as good as new. There was no damage done, nor any scar tissue evident on either lung. Absolutely no infection was apparent anywhere in the child's body.

In the next three months, Rex, Jr. gained forty-two pounds, more weight than most children his age normally gain in three years.

During the time of this personal emergency and concern for our son, we had been facing the problems of future meetings. We had communicated with the International Auditorium Association of America and other independent auditoriums across the nation, requesting a three-week period from each place during which we could hold nightly revival meetings. These engagements were to be held over the next three years. Out of the hundreds of auditoriums contacted, there were less than ten encouraging dates supplied. Some of these were for less than the three-week period we'd designated.

Since the meetings we were planning were to be city-wide campaigns, we felt it important to have a neutral location, apart from any local church. Seeing that auditoriums were not available, we then decided to investigate the idea of using a tent as an agreeable alternative. Now, suddenly, God made available the type of tent we needed.

When Oral Roberts was in St. Petersburg, we had heard he planned to purchase a new tent and his old one was for sale. We bought the tent and hired freight lines to take it to Daytona Beach. This was the place we'd had such a tragic experience before, but we weren't going to let that memory dampen our enthusiasm for the meeting in our new tent! Although this time the crowds were smaller, the Spirit of God was in the meetings and many souls were saved.

We moved to a site in Pensacola. Early fall is often an unfortunate time of year for weather changes on the Florida coast. Tropical storms frequently occur every day. It was true that year. Night after night we didn't know whether we could hold a meeting or not. Lashing winds and heavy rains sometimes ripped the tent badly. We would pull it down and patiently sew it up again. Then we'd rush to erect it in time for the evening service. All this was done in pouring rain, but by the help of God, we never missed a service.

Our testings didn't end. Following the rain came cold weather, making it equally difficult to hold tent meetings. People shuddered in the brisk temperatures. We kept praying the warmth of the Gospel message would more than make up for their physical discomfort.

Closing the Florida meetings, we headed for Dallas to spend Christmas with Maude Aimee's family, as was our custom. Then came January and we moved east to Augusta for meetings. There, also, it was really too cold for a tent service. We persevered and were rewarded by seeing many souls saved. It was an interesting discovery for us that, under such hardship conditions, the ones who did come really meant business. They were determined to find the Lord, and God rewarded them for their zeal. He met them there.

During the testings in these past meetings, we felt we could say with the Apostle Paul, "We are troubled on every side, yet not distressed; we are perplexed, but not in despair." For some reason God had allowed the meetings to have difficulties, yet, each time they came, we felt His presence with us.

Out of shadow, the Lord often leads us into His sunshine of blessing. Our next meeting was to be one of the greatest meetings we'd ever conducted in all our travels. It looked as if a twenty-four-hour-a-day revival had broken out within the city of Birmingham, Alabama, when our services began. All hours of the day or night, people kept coming to our door, asking us how to be saved and then requesting baptism afterwards, according to Scriptural admonition. Never before had we experienced such large scale outpouring of conviction, and gladly we stopped anything we might be doing in order to pray for these people who needed help.

Many unusual experiences occurred. One night, strangely burdened during an altar call, I pleaded for still one more person to respond. Minutes passed, and with a heavy heart I closed the meeting. Five days later at the Friday meeting, a brokenhearted woman stumbled to the altar and sobbed out a pathetic story. She and her husband had attended the previous Sunday service, when I'd held the service longer than usual to ask one more lost soul to turn to Christ. Afterwards, as they were leaving, her husband turned to her and admitted, "That last call was for me!"

Two days later that young man was killed. His wife now cried in her sorrow, telling me I had been right—someone had heard his last call. Tears came to my eyes as I thought how pride and stubbornness are tools Satan often uses to keep a soul from finding peace with God. There at the altar on that Friday evening, I explained how God offered comfort, and even more than that—forgiveness for her own sin and redemption through the blood of Jesus Christ. That night she surrendered to Christ, the One Who can bring the only true balm to a suffering heart.

The Birmingham meeting brought multiplied blessings. First, it had been exceptionally well organized with the help of Reverend Glenn V. Tingley, pastor of a large Christian and Missionary Alliance Church in Birmingham and a true servant of God. Both of us marveled how God met even the smallest detailed requirements in the arrangements. As I'd noticed in previous meetings when training our personal workers, if only 25 workers were ready to help with the counseling, then we were likely to have just that same number respond to the invitation. The Lord always anticipated our needs and worked things out accordingly.

And God blessed in another way. Costs for freight

companies' crating and hauling the tent had skyrocketed. In the long run, we knew we'd save money by buying our own trucks and moving the equipment ourselves. Miraculously, the Birmingham meetings had been so fruitful and moving that we even had the money to buy our own tractors and trailers. God supplied our need almost before we'd decided how the problem should be handled.

Somewhere I had once read that after a time of great blessing, we can usually expect the devil to attack more vigorously then ever. The heights of blessing when God had touched our son had been followed by conditions which easily could have led to discouragement. But that time of seeking a closer walk with the Lord had paid great dividends. By God's help, we'd remained faithful. In Birmingham and later in our meetings in Evansville, Indiana, the power of God was demonstrated more than ever before in our ministry.

God had a plan for our lives. As we waited on Him and worked to bring lost souls into His kingdom, He was working in His season to bring that plan about.

"And, behold, I am with thee, and will keep thee in all places whither thou goest, and will bring thee again into this land; for I will not leave thee, until I have done that which I have spoken to thee of." (Genesis 28:15)

CHAPTER 14

A strong sense of danger hit me. I couldn't seem to shake it. It was like receiving a telegram from God—not a visible telegram, but a clear signal that could not be ignored.

It all began during our meeting in Owensboro, Kentucky. We had been there two weeks. This was a hard meeting, completely the reverse of the two previous thrilling ones. But temporary discouragement was never allowed to get us down. Already we were eager to begin the next set of services in Convington, Kentucky. It was when I was working out the final details of the Covington meeting that I felt the danger signal. I didn't know what it was all about but decided to investigate.

I flew to Covington to check the situation there. The local minister drove me to the lot which was to be the tent site. It seemed all right. Cooperation in the city had been satisfactory. Radio arrangements were exceptionally agreeable. I couldn't find a single thing to make me uneasy. But I still felt it. I knew there was danger—just as surely as if there'd been big signs there, with red letters and flashing lights.

That afternoon I flew back to Owensboro and announced, "We're extending this meeting another week."

"Why?" came the immediate question from everyone.

I didn't know why. There were no words to explain. But long ago I'd learned to obey the "still, small voice" within me. Even though my inclinations and common sense told me it was silly to wait, still I had to obey.

The following week the meetings continued. I could feel the question behind everyone's eyes, "Well, what's the reason?" God had put me on the spot. But I wouldn't budge.

The third day of that week, miles away in Covington, the skies grew dark, the air still. Then with a roar the cyclone struck. Destruction was everywhere. The grounds where our tent and trailers would have stood were churned by the winds—torn so badly that even the cyclone fences were leveled. Had our equipment been there, everything would have been demolished.

When the news reached me, I felt no surprise. Shock and sorrow for the people there. . .but no surprise that my danger signal was real. I could only praise the Lord over and over that the contact was clear between God and me.

The Lord has such a wonderful way of leading His children. It's quite a contrast to how the devil drives his followers. God doesn't force us to obey. He leads us by His Word and that "still, small voice" within. Sometimes we're so busy telling God the way we want things, we fail to hear what He's trying to tell us. "Be still and know that I am God." These instructions can lead us to His protection, His guidance, His safety.

While we were in Owensboro, the time arrived for six-year-old Rex, Jr. to start school. So it was in the hills of Kentucky he trudged away for his first day of studying, and he loved it. But he could only attend there for two weeks. Our next meeting was in Terre Haute, Indiana, and there again our eldest son got in two and a half weeks of classes before we had to move on. More changes of schools were to follow. Despite the fact he had such a short time in each place, he appeared to thrive. All the children he met promptly became good friends. His first report cards showed straight A's. We breathed a sigh of relief, for clearly God was taking care of a problem which could have been most difficult. In His wisdom, the Lord was smoothing things out all along the way.

Weather once again challenged us. In Terre Haute, we battled storms but still had a good meeting. It was getting too cold for northern tent meetings, so again we headed south. The Jacksonville temperatures, by all expectations, should have been balmy. But winter penetrated even into Florida that year. The temperature dropped as low as 28 degrees, entirely too chilly for sitting in a tent. We bought huge electric blowers to make the audience more comfortable, but still we found ourselves playing our instruments while bundled in heavy coats and gloves.

Closing the Jacksonville meeting early, we headed for Texas. During the Christmas season our plans were completed for another series of meetings on the West Coast, beginning with a revival in Oakland's Neighborhood Church and proceeding up to Seattle, Washington, for dedicatory services in the brand new Calvary Temple there.

Unfortunately, after Christmas Rex, Jr. came down with chicken pox. Despite this, we managed to get him in shape to make the trip west. Then, the day we arrived in Oakland, Donnie, too, broke out with chicken pox! People living in well-regulated comfortable homes often bewail the misfortune of children's diseases. I'm sure they can't imagine what it's like coping with similar conditions while out on the road. Those trying days of recuperation finally passed, and the boys bounced back to health once more. Rex, Jr. even spent five days in Oakland schools before we were ready to leave.

But the minor annoyances pursued us to Portland. Rex, Jr. blossomed red again—this time with measles. It was only a short while before he passed it on to Donnie. Though traveling—and even living—became much more difficult, we managed, and went on to enjoy splendid services in Portland and Salem, Oregon, before we moved to Seattle.

In Oakland, California, just before we'd left, I'd answered the telephone and been surprised to hear the voice of a dear friend.

"Rex, this is Cap Stabbert. You'll never guess what I'm doing now!"

That voice brought back memories to me. The last time I had seen Cap Stabbert was when I was with Billy Graham in a Youth for Christ meeting in Seattle. Cap had been the organist for the service. He was a well-known Seattle businessman, and I'd been deeply impressed with his zeal for winning souls.

"You're right, Cap. Knowing you—it's bound to be something dynamic. What's new?"

"Rex, I'm sailing the waters of Alaska!"

Cap went on to explain what had happened in the intervening years since I'd seen him. Willis Shank, director of the Youth for Christ movement in Seattle, had felt God's call to the mission field. He resigned his position, bought a boat and set off to Alaska to minister to the Indian tribes on the islands. These people had no churches or pastors, and Willis felt an intense burden for their souls. Above all else, he knew they needed God. In a few short months he'd built a church in Alaska. Then he went back to Seattle to finish the arrangements for getting his boat.

When Shank was returning to Alaska to dedicate his new church, the Northwest Airlines plane in which he was flying failed to clear the top of one of the mountains. It crashed in the wilderness. Every occupant of the plane was killed. Most of the passengers and crew were mutilated beyond recognition. When the rescue party arrived, they were surprised and deeply touched to see one body lying apart from the wreckage, yards from the others. It had no mar or bruise on it. Nearby, an open Bible was mute testimony of the man's occupation. On the flyleaf of the cover they read the name—Willis Shank, and on the opposite page they saw the words: "Saved by the Blood of the Crucified One."

When news of this tragedy reached Cap Stabbert, he mortgaged his home and sold his business. Then he purchased the boat, naming it *The Willis Shank.* Cap had dedicated himself to doing the work Willis Shank would have done.

I was deeply touched by Cap's story. Having heard the Humbards were on the West Coast, he had called to ask us to accompany him on a trip to Alaska. Cap seemed to feel our music and preaching would bring great blessing to the Indian tribes. The work was a true missionary venture. There was no financial support. We would have to bear our own expenses.

I thought for a few seconds, recalling how good God had been to us. Recently, money had come in unusually well. It seemed as if this were the reason God had allowed us the little extra. He had prepared the way so we could make this trip. Quickly I gave Cap our answer, "O.K., we'll go."

The following weeks were busy ones. We carried on services while at the same time we prepared for the six-week Alaskan tour. My wife was worn out from nursing the boys through their childhood illnesses. In the midst of it all, she had continued to participate nightly in the services and daily in the broadcasts. Looking forward to the tour certainly boosted her morale and stimulated both of us spiritually. But we knew we'd be serving in some primitive areas, and this would be a further strain on her health. I kept wishing she could have rested a bit more before we left.

The train on which we were to go to Vancouver cleared Customs and crossed the border into Canada. Miles had passed, with the train moving north, when I received a telegram. It stated that the boy who was driving the truck loaded with our instruments had been held at the border until the owner of the load could sign for customs clearance. I had to get off the train, find a taxi, and go back 30 miles to clear up the difficulty. Then I rode the truck up to Vancouver just in time to make the sailing. We met at the docks and together boarded *The Prince Ruppert,* a vessel owned by the Canadian Steamship Line. We began the first leg of our journey.

Cap Stabbert and his family met us in Ketchikan, the colorful Alaskan town where *The Willis Shank* was berthed. The first major chore was transferring our instruments and luggage to the ship, which was to be our home for the next five weeks. As we stowed the gear, Maude Aimee came in for some teasing. In the confusion of packing, her shoes had been mixed up with the instrument cases and these were sealed by government order. Since the seals couldn't be broken on that portion of the luggage until we boarded *The Willis Shank,* she had been stuck for a week with only the shoes on her feet—naturally, the high-heeled, impractical kind!

The twelve people in our party joined *The Willis Shank* crew of nineteen to make up the total group. For maximum efficiency, it was necessary for each one on board to do his part in caring for himself and the ship. The work was divided. We drew lots for our assignments, and Maude Aimee and I were given the task of dishwashing. I abruptly discovered washing dishes three times a day for 31 people is no easy job. It took two hours after each meal to finish up. By the end of the trip we both agreed if we never washed another dish in our lifetimes, we'd probably still be ahead of most people in experience!

Our itinerary took us into the most humble villages. We made stops at all the little islands, holding afternoon services each day and then traveling on to the next port for an evening service. Occasionally, when we couldn't find an adequate auditorium, the meetings were held on shipboard. Many of those people who listened so intently had never before heard the name of Jesus. Though most of them were English-speaking, occasionally we used an interpreter when necessary. The Indians—young and old—delighted in the music, whether they could understand the words or not. Rex, Jr. had been wanting to play the cowbells, so during the trip we set them up for him. He soon learned to play them with considerable skill, and the people laughed happily at the antics of this little boy. After hearing our songs, most of the natives wanted records. If they couldn't buy, they always found a way of trading something to obtain them.

The Indians listened to the sermons with quiet attention, almost with awe. Usually an entire tribe would attend the service, and one night more than 100 people came forward to claim salvation in Jesus Christ.

Communism penetrated even that area. In one town where we docked, we discovered there were only two Christians, and these were not permitted to worship in public. Everyone else there claimed to be a Communist. Though we were not allowed to preach or even tell them the wonderful news of Jesus' love, we still entertained about 40 children who had come to the boat and waited eagerly to hear us sing. How burdened our hearts were for those lost ones in that town, blinded by sin and determined to spread their godlessness.

In those weeks we ministered through much of Southern Alaska and Western Canada. Reaching our northernmost point, we sailed back down the coast toward Seattle, once again taking the instruments ashore in rowboats at each stop we made. Often we had to wait until after midnight for the tide to change before the Indians could shove the boats out through the breakers. The only accident in the entire trip happened when a wave struck a boat and tossed Wayne's bass fiddle into the sea. Fortunately it floated and we got it back quickly, without damage. Despite the difficulties and hazards, God filled our hearts with the joy of spreading the Gospel and brought us safely back home.

The six wonderful weeks ended. We stopped in Vancouver, British Columbia, for a Youth for Christ rally and finally headed for Seattle. It had been a great trip. We'd seen souls saved. We'd watched people—who had never before heard the Gospel—hungrily listen and then ask for more. We kept remembering one little Indian boy who braved unbelievable hardships to come to hear the story of Jesus Christ, and once having heard, kept returning over and over again. He was one of many who thirsted for the Living Water.

We had seen the fulfillment of God's promise: "So shall my word be that goeth forth out of my mouth: it shall not return unto me void, but it shall accomplish that which I please, and it shall prosper in the thing whereto I sent it." (Isaiah 55:11)

"Delight thyself also in the Lord; and He shall give thee the desires of thine heart. Commit thy way unto the Lord; trust also in Him; and He shall bring it to pass." (Psalm 37: 4, 5)

CHAPTER 15

We were bubbling with stories of our Alaskan trip. Eagerly we returned to take up our scheduled meetings—moving first to Birmingham, Alabama, and then to Evansville, Indiana. Both had been sites of fruitful meetings in years past. Now we were also to share with them our enthusiasm for what God can do in outposts where people are longing, pleading for spiritual food!

Here in America, where churches are found on almost every corner, we often fail to realize the privilege of hearing God's Word preached regularly, of having fellowship with other Christians. I think we often forget the value of our freedom and opportunity. And, perhaps, if we took advantage of the opportunities for God's work more often than we do, we'd see a greater harvest of souls. In those services in Birmingham and Evansville, we urged people to seek God first, to let their souls prosper—not just their businesses.

Spring had come, and South Bend, Indiana, was next on the agenda. One day I was surveying a lot there on which we planned to set up the tent, when I noticed another man surveying the very same lot. We started talking. It was interesting to me to learn he was an advance man for Ringling

Brothers, Barnum and Bailey Circus, nationally advertised as "The Greatest Show on Earth."

"My job," he explained, "is to check the lot, order hay for it if it happens to be muddy, and just be sure all is clear for tomorrow's set-up. Three other guys traveled up here before me to make the previous arrangements."

He glanced at me inquiringly and then added, "What department are you in, for your show?"

Laughing at his terminology, I replied, "All of them. I rent the lot, take out the permits, make the arrangements for electricity, transportation, advertising, radio broadcasts, and telephone lines for on-the-spot pick-ups; and then I solicit the cooperation of the local ministerial association and arrange for ushers and personal workers to counsel with converts in our meetings. When the tent arrives, I help drive the stakes, stretch the canvas and build the platform. On opening night I'm behind the pulpit, acting as master-of-ceremonies."

As I finished, I could see his eyes getting bigger and bigger. Then he said, almost as if talking to himself, "One guy can't do all that!"

I chuckled and kicked at the clump of dirt beside me. "Well, how can I explain it...I guess I'm kind of like that bumble bee over there. The scientist examines it carefully. He measures its wing spread, weighs it and says, 'According to aeronautical rules, it can't fly.' But the bee doesn't know that. So he flies anyway."

I went on to explain about the part God plays in all this—the important part. He nodded when I finished, thinking deeply.

"You know," he said slowly, "maybe you're the ones, after all, who have the 'Greatest Show on Earth.' "

The circus was due in South Bend shortly after we started

the meeting. On the morning it arrived, I got up at four o'clock and went down to watch them set up. I was curious to see how they did it. Their tent looked gigantic. It was so much bigger than our "Gospel Big Top" that I knew I'd learn something. I watched them hoist the tent and then set up their expensive equipment. All the time I kept thinking, "God's work shouldn't be second best to anything. The Lord's people should have the best. We ought to be able to worship in the finest tent money can buy."

Right then I decided to go back home and pray about the matter. For a long time we'd needed a new tent. Storms had damaged the one we had, and it had been mended and remended. I knew it ought to be discarded.

I contacted one of the biggest tent companies in Chicago and then drove up to talk to them about the kind of tent I would like to have. Our present tent seated three thousand people, but I dreamed of one that seated at least six thousand.

The men started figuring. They drew up blueprints and finally gave me the cost of the tent I'd described. The final figure was $21,000. That was a lot of money. I knew there was no use going into such an undertaking as this, unless it was God's will. Before we left South Bend, I'd prayed about it a lot.

Usually when something big faced us, we tried "putting out a fleece to God," just as Gideon had done in the Old Testament. I had to know for sure that God was in this transaction. I told the Lord that if at least one thousand dollars was received in the Sunday night service, I would take it as His will to go ahead. Then, on faith, we'd order the new tent.

That night I explained to the people who were gathered for the service that we were sorely in need of a new tent. I told them I had "put out a fleece to God." I didn't beg or plead,

115

and I was careful not to mention the specific sum I'd prayed about. I merely asked them to put into the offering plates just what God prompted them to give. When the offering was counted that night, it contained exactly $1,060. We ordered the tent.

Now we had a goal to work for. The down payment was arranged to be $6,000. That amount had to come in fast, for it was due very soon. We started working hard in promotion. Our friends in South Bend helped tremendously, and before we could believe it ourselves, God had provided the total sum of the down payment. We were one step nearer to having our brand new tent.

The South Bend meeting was memorable in another way. There I witnessed the most heartbreaking—but still, triumphant—incident. It was one I will remember all my life.

One day before the meetings were to start, we moved the trailers into the South Bend trailer camp which was to be our home for the next few weeks. Out from behind a shed popped a grubby, freckled-faced lad.

"Help ya, mister?" he asked brightly.

"Thanks, son, but I think you're much too small for this."

"Oh, no, sir," he protested, "I'm strong. . .I'm real strong." He picked up the nearby blocks and hauled them into place to prove it.

"What's your name," I asked, after admiring his efforts.

"Lloyd, sir. What's yours?"

"Rex Humbard."

"Rex. . .I've never known anyone named that before. Could I call you Rex? I'd like that."

"Go right ahead. I'd like that, too."

Ragged as he was, he had such a kind heart and disposition that in a short time we all became attached to him. As he warmed to us, he revealed his tragic story. Young Lloyd had lost his mother, brother and sister when a train hit the car in which they were riding. Even before that, his homelife had been wretched. His parents were separated because his father couldn't leave liquor alone. Now, after the death of most of his family, he was compelled to live with his dad in a beat-up, old trailer at the edge of the trailer camp. He knew none of the luxuries of life and pitifully few of the necessities.

Lloyd managed to get enough money for food by mowing lawns, running errands and doing odd jobs around the neighborhood. The joys in his life had been meager, but when he saw us putting up our tent, his eyes grew bright.

"Rex, what would it cost me to come to your meeting in the tent? If I work real hard, maybe I could earn enough."

Those big, brown eyes reached right down to my heart. "It's free to everyone, Lloyd. You can come all you want—every night, if you wish. I'll have a special seat right down here in front, just for you."

From that first service, little Lloyd's chair was never empty. Eagerly he listened to the sermons and drank in the beauty of the music. One night I saw him walk determinedly to the altar. He knew what it was all about. He wanted his sins forgiven. He wanted the Lord Jesus to save him.

From that night on, we noticed he was hungry to learn more of the Word of God. I gave him a Bible for his very own, and he tucked it under his arm and carried it proudly into the service. Though he was only eleven years old, his heart had been deeply touched. Never before had he known such happiness. No longer did we see the wistful, woebegone look on his face. His smile became a beam. Lack of money, lack of love would never again defeat him. He now had the love of God.

One day as I was going into a drug store to place a long distance telephone call, Lloyd rode by on his raggedy old bike.

"Hi, Rex," he yelled, "going to have a film tonight?"

"Yes, Lloyd, a real good Bible film."

He smiled. "I'll be seeing you. I'll be right on the front row."

Not thirty minutes later, little Lloyd did make it up to the front row—the front row before the Throne of God. He saw the Saviour he had so recently accepted.

For him there was to be no more heartache and sorrow, no more caring for a drunken father who didn't care for him, no more begging for work to give him a few pennies for a bite to eat. A carelessly driven automobile-carrier truck had turned the corner. The driver didn't see the lad on his old bike, and Lloyd was rolled between the truck and the curb. In that instant, Lloyd felt a quick stab of pain and then smiled as he looked into his Saviour's face. For him, "to live is Christ, but to die is gain."

"Trust in the Lord with all thine heart; and lean not unto thine own understanding. In all thy ways acknowledge Him, and He shall direct thy paths." (Proverbs 3:5, 6)

CHAPTER 16

We had been warned against holding a meeting in Chicago. Advice was that people in Chicago just weren't interested in revival meetings. But we found it necessary to stay in the vicinity for a short time in order to work out details for our new tent. A little extra time and care in planning would be rewarded in end results. We decided to disregard those warnings and hold a meeting in Chicago anyway. If only one soul was reached, it would be worth all our efforts there.

We erected the tent on one of the main thoroughfares. It was a great meeting. The tent was packed every night. People responded to altar calls. Later, in talking with those who came forward, we were astonished to learn many of them had never before heard the name of Jesus! In this land of ours with its many churches, it seemed impossible. Older people, some in their seventies and eighties, came forward and prayed, admitting they had never prayed before and wanted to learn how. We explained how they could be born again—born into God's family. And then what a miracle it was to see them, so close to eternity, finally find salvation and joy in Jesus Christ. Now they were ready to meet Him in glory, to dwell with Him forever.

Chicago was a city ripe for the Lord. Necessity had forced

us to stay there, but God had made the opportunity. And He gave us souls for His Kingdom.

* * * * * *

Everytime I had to build a platform for the tent and then had to assist in tearing it down again at the end of a seventeen-day meeting, I knew there must be a better way to handle the situation. In my mind's eye I could see a beautiful trailer with sides that folded down to form a platform. It could be permanently wired for telephone lines to handle radio programs, as well as for electricity for lights and instruments. Now was the time, with the new tent under construction, to check to see if such a trailer was possible.

In Chicago, I consulted a trailer company and described what I had in mind. Immediately they set to work on blueprints to iron out details. Now I was certain it was possible to get the platform-trailer van I'd longed for. It could be wheeled in and made ready for services in minutes. On it we'd carry all our instruments, which by this time included an organ, a piano, a harp, a vibra-harp, cowbells and sleighbells, accordions, the bass fiddle, and electric guitars along with other guitars—alone almost enough to fill the trailer. We had also been able to purchase another tractor in Chicago, and this would be ready to pull the new trailer when it was completed. To our joy, the Lord provided the down payments on all this equipment. We dedicated it to Him and knew He would not fail to supply our needs each month, when the payments came due.

* * * * * *

Eleven schools, plus an extended trip through Alaska—that had been the schedule for Rex, Jr.'s first school year.

Perhaps, for the first year, it hadn't mattered much. But now as we faced his continuing studies, we knew we couldn't move him around every seventeen days. We had to locate at some central point where Maude Aimee could stay with the children. Hot Springs seemed to be the logical place. My son would be attending the same school I had attended, and my wife could continue working for the Lord in the Gospel Temple, where my sister Ruth and her husband, Louis Davidson, were located.

When my family was comfortably settled, I rushed back to Gary, Indiana, to begin the next meeting. Those seventeen days apart seemed endless. We weren't used to being separated, and Maude Aimee was discovering that bearing the full responsibility of two active little boys was more of a problem than she'd anticipated. They tried to be helpful, however. Rex, Jr. considered himself the man of the house when I was away and took his duties seriously. My wife had little trouble with discipline.

Because our next meeting was in Jonesboro, Arkansas, only one hundred miles away, I rejoined the family for a couple of days, on the way down. The family managed to come over for the services each Friday, as soon as school was out, and returned to Hot Springs early Monday mornings. Services in Little Rock followed that meeting. But the weather eventually turned colder. The advent of snow compelled us to pull down the tent and return to Hot Springs where we held revival services until the Christmas season.

All this time I was wrestling with the problem of how to mortgage the new tent, now well on its way to completion. But locating the financing was no easy task. Banks weren't interested in loaning money on a tent. It just wasn't considered good collateral. What could banking institutions do with a tent, if they had to repossess? I was meeting defeat every way I turned, but I hadn't given up. God never steered me wrong, and I was convinced God had the problem well in hand, even if I had not yet received the answer.

Just then, we received a call from our good friends, Earl and Pauline Sexauer in Oakland, California, inviting us back to the Neighborhood Church for one month of meetings during January, 1952. It seemed a long hard trip to make, just for a month's meetings, but, as in everything else we did, before making a decision, we took the matter to God. The answer was clear and sure. God wanted us to go.

The meetings at the Neighborhood Church were spiritually powerful. How we enjoyed those days with the Sexauers! We stayed in their home, and the time spent with these wonderful friends seemed to pass so quickly. Years later we were to look back on this companionship and praise God for providing it.

One sunny afternoon I was standing in an Oakland bank, cashing a check, when inspiration struck me. The friendliness of the teller may have prompted the impulse, but the Lord was surely behind it.

"Who is the head man in your Loan Department?" I inquired.

The teller mentioned his name and then asked politely, "Would you like to talk to him? Right this way."

When I entered the office, I explained my business. "I'd like to borrow fifteen thousand dollars."

The manager nodded slightly and questioned, "And what about security?"

I explained the money was to buy a tent. We would have to give them a mortgage on it and obtain insurance to cover it in case of accident. We'd been advised our tent was ready, but still we hadn't made proper arrangements for financing it.

The banker paused a moment and then said thoughtfully, "I think I can help you." Dialing the number of a friend of his, an insurance broker, he confidently inquired, "Would you insure a tent?"

To my delight, the reply was affirmative. The insurance agent hurried to the bank, and before long all necessary arrangements were finished. Up to this time, all the figures quoted to me on insurance rates had been around $1,200. Now this firm offered us insurance for half that sum. Agreeing on the remaining business details for financing the tent, the bank officials offered me an interest figure which almost staggered me. It was the lowest I'd ever heard.

While I was waiting there for the entire transaction to be completed, one startling thought struck my mind. This had been the reason God told us so clearly to drive across country to California! I had been worrying and fussing about financing the tent, and all along God had arranged it here in Oakland.

Our check was ready to pick up the next day, and immediately we sent it to the tent company. Our "Gospel Big Top" was on the way for delivery!

Houston, Texas was the spot picked for the debut of our grand new tent and platform-trailer. We knew it would be a great meeting, but it exceeded our expectations. Now we were looking to God for greater results than ever before, for a harvest of souls that we'd claim for His glory. What a boost to our faith that addition had been!

Moving to Birmingham, Alabama, then to Dallas, and on to Oklahoma City for splendid services showed us how valuable our new equipment really was. Right about that time, schools closed and summer vacations began. This meant my wife and sons could join me from their home in Dallas, where Maude Aimee had moved the house trailer before Christmas and Rex, Jr. had been in classes the second semester of his school year.

Kansas City was the site of our next meeting. It was when we were deeply engrossed in these services that I got a letter from Reverend Paul Sorenson of Canton, Ohio, asking us to consider bringing the tent there. That seemed to be a long way to travel from Kansas City with all the equipment we now had to transport. After praying for guidance about the matter, we were in accord that Canton was the place to which God wanted us to go.

Canton *was* the place! Crowds turned out every night. It was a wonderful revival. About midway through the campaign, two newspaper reporters from Akron, twenty-five miles north, stopped by our tent by accident on their way to cover another story. They had intended to visit Meyers Lake Park, a resort in Canton which was featuring a famous name band. Once the men arrived at our tent, however, they stayed for the entire service. They could see for themselves what God was doing, and they went back to Akron to turn out an article on us for the *Akron Beacon Journal*. Soon people were driving down from Akron to Canton every night.

As usual toward the closing nights of a current meeting, I was scheduled to move on for advance work elsewhere. I flew to Baltimore, Maryland, and checked final preliminary arrangements for erection of the "Gospel Big Top." Baltimore had donated the use of the city park, an excellent location right on the Philadelphia highway. Ministers in that area enthusiastically looked forward to sponsoring the services. All the plans were complete.

I flew back to the Akron-Canton airport where Wayne was waiting to meet me.

"Wayne, we're not going to Baltimore next."

Astonishment showed in his face. "Why not? I thought everything was great there."

"It's strange, Wayne. I can't see any logical reason for not going on to Baltimore. I just don't feel right about it."

We were both subdued for a few moments. Then I gave him what seemed a strange request. "How about driving me up toward the center of Akron?"

Readily he wheeled the car around in that direction. As we left the airport area, we passed the gigantic Rubber Bowl, Akron's famous stadium, and Derby Downs, home of the world renowned Soap Box Derby, which Akron annually sponsors.

I looked up and an idea hit me. "Wayne, wouldn't it be terrific to set up the tent there near Derby Downs? What a place for a meeting!"

"Derby Downs, Rex?" Wayne sounded shocked, but then he toyed with the idea. "Yeh, that's the place."

"Turn around. . .let's find the man in charge."

Back at Akron Airport I met Shorty Fulton, who welcomed us cordially. He had read the news story of the Humbards in the Beacon Journal. He was impressed. In those moments I had complete assurance that this was where our next meeting was going to be. The tents were down, the trucks were already packed. We'd bring them to the Rubber Capital of the World—Akron, Ohio.

"The Lord is good unto them that wait for Him, to the soul that seeketh Him." (Lamentations 3:25)

CHAPTER 17

No spot in the entire country was harder than Akron for making arrangements to set up a tent. There was no city ordinance covering erection of tents. Permission for each individual application had to be obtained from Akron City Council. Time was consumed waiting for them to convene.

On Tuesday morning I went before the City Council, requesting permission to locate on city property on Triplett Boulevard. I also asked for permits to cover all aspects of the meeting. The Council voted and passed an ordinance permitting the "Gospel Big Top" to be erected on the selected site near Akron Airport. Next, our equipment was transported from Canton to Akron, and by Saturday night the tent was up, the meeting was open, and God's work had begun.

Our meetings were always sponsored by local churches. Twelve fundamental churches sponsored the meeting in Canton. A number of Baltimore churches had volunteered to support us there. But the significant part about the Akron meeting was that it had been arranged in such a short time that there was no opportunity to contact local churches. God knew I could not establish a permanent work if I had sponsoring groups, and He held the future.

Many Akron people had traveled to Canton to hear us in

our previous meeting. Several of these came to me requesting we invite Kathryn Kuhlman as a guest speaker. She had held meetings in many cities surrounding Akron, though never in Akron itself. Her services always drew fantastic crowds.

When our tent opened in Akron, again so many people made this same request that I decided to go to Pittsburgh and hear Miss Kuhlman myself. When I did, I was impressed—not by the crowds or the facilities, but because she gave all the glory to the Lord. People were changed, and the changes in their thinking resulted in action. Burdens were lifted, bodies were healed, souls were saved.

Despite the fact we'd attended two of her meetings in Pittsburgh and witnessed the huge crowds there, we were still unprepared for what happened when she came to Akron to speak in our tent. Kathryn Kuhlman was scheduled for the 11 a.m. service. By 6:00 in the morning I couldn't get into my own tent, which seated 6,000. There were 25 circles of people surrounding the tent on the outside. Over 1,500 of those who had attended our meeting on Saturday evening had spent the entire night in the tent in order to have choice seats for the Kuhlman meeting the next morning.

Newspapers estimated the audience that Sunday as being 18,000. The service began at 7:30 in the morning and lasted until 1:30 in the afternoon. Over 1,150 people knelt in the sawdust to pray and give their hearts to Jesus Christ. Kathryn Kuhlman was invited back the next Sunday morning, and again we saw a harvest of souls.

Wherever God is given free rein to work, wherever faith is great and God blesses abundantly, Satan tries to step in to defeat God's power for good. Kathryn Kuhlman and our family had occasion to remember that corollary and cling to Jesus' words: "Blessed are ye, when men shall revile you, and persecute you, and shall say all manner of evil against you falsely, for my sake. Rejoice and be exceeding glad: for great is your reward in heaven: for so persecuted they the prophets which were before you."

Before many days passed, local newspapers were carrying stories designed to damage the work we were trying to do. If opposition had come from the secular world, it would have been easier to bear. But it came from a minister—one who, years earlier in 1944, had invited the Humbards to appear as special guests in his church. He had greeted us warmly then, marveling publicly about how wonderful it was to see an entire family working so hard for the Lord. But in the intervening years he had gone on record as opposing Kathryn Kuhlman's work. When she visited our tent, hundreds of people flocked there to be saved. Suddenly this minister changed his mind about the Humbards and discredited us as he had discredited Kathryn Kuhlman. To the public, he let what appeared to be professional jealousy give way to "guilt by association." Now he was giving interviews to the Akron papers vowing to "run us out of town."

The Akron Ministerial Association had had no objection to our meetings. The city officials had been most kind. In contrast to this minister, the civic officials—Mayor Charles Slussor; Marvin Davis, the service director; and Russell Byrd, chairman of the City Council—were very gracious. So, a conflict with a local minister over what appeared to be a non-Biblical issue brought me deep regret. I promised the Lord I'd not speak against him, for he remained in a position of a servant of the Lord. I could only commit the situation to God and pray that no souls would be hurt or prevented from finding Christ because of it.

Days passed and a new logistics problem confronted me. Unfortunately, the tent had been placed in a location which added to traffic congestion and neighborhood commotion. There were insufficient facilities to handle the enormous crowds which unexpectedly were attending the meetings. The neighbors near the area started complaining, and I couldn't blame them. I had no idea that such a situation would develop. Immediately we sensed the only solution would be to move the tent to a spot where crowds would not disturb. In the midst of making this decision, I got a telephone call. Considering the congestion, the Mayor was contacting me to say, very kindly, that he was forced to revoke our present permits. All the Akron officials voiced their regret at having to take such an action.

But God had not yet told us where to go. We prayed earnestly, and we didn't have long to wait for His leading. A few days before this, a real estate executive influential in the community had "hit the sawdust trail." His name was O. Clare Conlan. For forty years he'd been active at City Hall. He had been Potentate of the Shrine and had served on the Board of Directors of the Akron Automobile Association. Everywhere in political and social circles he was well-known. Mr. Conlan now offered us his services. At his own suggestion, he visited the mayor to testify: "I've been saved at these meetings. The Humbards' ministry has done a great deal for me personally. I want them to stay in Akron."

The mayor took Mr. Conlan to a special Council meeting and his testimony in that group turned the tide. The Akron City Council voted to permit us to erect our tent near Derby Downs. We could use the facilities of the Rubber Bowl, and no neighbors would be there to be bothered by crowds.

This was the fulfillment of my dream that first day when I stood with Wayne at the airport. I found myself so choked up I could only mumble, "Thank you, Lord. This is your way."

The Council suggested we move the tent by Monday, if possible. It was then Friday. We decided we could do even better than that, with the help of the Lord. At the Friday evening service and on our late radio program that day, we enlisted volunteers to help take down the tent and re-erect it on the following day. Hundreds of people responded. We worked all night and all the next day. By the time the Saturday night service rolled around, the tent was ready, standing imposingly at Derby Downs.

It was a testimony to God's power. This had been a task which normally required at least four or five days of work. The electric company and crews had declared it couldn't be done. We weren't the ones who made it possible. It was the Lord.

Originally we set up the tent for a seventeen-day meeting, but that time was extended to five weeks. We couldn't cut off the services while daily it was demonstrated that people were eager to find Jesus Christ. During this five-week period Kathryn Kuhlman returned for special services each Sunday morning. All during the week under our own ministry we also saw hundreds more give their lives to the Lord.

The fruitful Akron meeting closed. The "Gospel Big Top" was again pulled down and this time moved to Cleveland. But it wasn't long before we realized our audiences were composed of familiar faces. The same ones we had seen in Akron were driving thirty miles north to the Cleveland meetings. We might just as well have been back in Akron. The majority of people came from there. A quiet voice told me over and over again I was being held in Akron for a purpose. I was not through in that Ohio city.

Three different suggestions were made about our immediate future. Dad Humbard felt we ought to take the tent to Florida for the winter. Clement wanted to go to California to conduct a series of meetings on the West Coast. I thought we should stay in Akron. This last suggestion seemed the most impractical of all, for I didn't quite know how to manage it. Payments on the tent, trucks and equipment would continue through the winter. We had the tent, but Akron was too cold for tent meetings. Regardless, I felt the Lord speaking to me about Akron.

A thought struck me. How about renting a local theater and carrying on with radio work in the Akron area? The burden for Akron which I carried I couldn't understand. Nor could I dislodge it. Wayne, too, felt God's leading and urged that we stay despite the obvious difficulties.

A preliminary inquiry revealed the Copley Theater, one of Akron's newest theaters, had felt the pinch of television and was available for rental for a six-month period. The managers would accept an offer of $1,000 per month. We prayed, and the deal was settled. We started advertising and broadcasting our plans. We'd be in Akron for six months. The Copley Auditorium seated almost a thousand, and from the very beginning our meetings were crowded every night.

Housing for my family became another concern, and thus, a matter for prayer. Because of the severe Akron winters, for the first time Maude Aimee and I decided to find a house to rent, rather than use our little trailer. We put an advertisement in the paper and checked on many homes, but none met our needs. Then one day a woman called to tell me her neighbors were going to Florida for the winter. They would probably want to rent their home. While she walked across the street to talk to them, I waited at the phone. The couple readily agreed to let me have the place for six months, despite the fact we had two lively boys. God had wonderfully provided once again.

A month after the Akron meetings got underway for the second time, Dad and Mom left for Arkansas. Soon afterwards, Clem asked for six weeks off. But our crowds kept increasing. Wayne and I kept busy looking after the meetings. The radio broadcasts more than doubled in number. Every night WAKR carried the Humbards' program, in addition to our morning programs on that station and on

WCUE.

My sister Ruth and her husband, Louis Davidson, arrived to hold special revivals for us. Louis was an instant success with the Akron audiences. We persuaded them to extend their visit.

Then, suddenly, I was alone. God seemed to be making me preach and handle the other details as well, whether I liked it or not. Wayne had worked in a temporary job in Cleveland while we held the services in Copley Auditorium. Faithfully he returned every night and each weekend for the services. But now his employer was offering to accompany Wayne and Leona to Miami for a few weeks. Naturally they felt it was a great opportunity, and we wanted them to take advantage of it.

That fateful month of December, 1952, was one I'll never forget. I started tossing in bed at night. My mind was full of questions. Should I stay in Akron? Should I start a church and become a pastor? I couldn't believe what the Lord was saying to me.

I argued, "But Lord, I'm not a preacher. I'm more a business manager. I just couldn't be a pastor of a congregation. I don't know how. But Lord. . .whatever you want me to do, I want to win souls."

In the morning I questioned my wife, "What do you think about it? How do you feel about staying in Akron?"

Maude Aimee didn't want to influence me in my decision. "Rex," she replied, "whatever you decide to do is all right with me. I want you to do God's will. Wherever you go, or whatever God wants you to do, that will be all right with me."

The following night I was restless again. I found myself pleading with God, saying my whole life was bound up with the tent and our evangelistic work across the country. That was something He had shown me I was capable of doing.

Mom and Dad and Clement had left all the business details to me. I didn't want to let them down.

Thus it went, night after night. I felt like Jacob as he wrestled with the angel. Worn out and knowing I had to take time alone to commune with God—to know His perfect will, I decided not to schedule meetings during Christmas week.

The Christmas season was particularly happy for us. We'd worked hard to get baskets ready for needy families. People had brought in canned goods, and we added chickens to give the folks a real Christmas feast. To us, this was the true spirit of Christmas, and it blessed us as much as it did those thankful families whose eyes brightened when they saw the gifts. At our last service we passed out bags of candy, nuts and fruit to the little children. It was a real old-fashioned Christmas.

On Christmas day I finally made my decision. The week before had been saved exclusively for the Lord. I took time to talk with Him. When finally I prayed, "God, if this is what you want me to do, give me the answer through your Word," my Bible fell open to Matthew 8:26: "And He saith unto them, Why are ye fearful, O ye of little faith? Then He arose, and rebuked the winds and the sea; and there was a great calm."

And a great calm came upon my heart. I had found my answer.

I prayed, "Lord, forgive me for my lack of faith. Never let me be guilty of it again." Then I added, "Yes, Lord, I'll stay."

"But without faith it is impossible to please Him: for he that cometh to God must believe that He is, and that He is a rewarder of them that diligently seek Him." (Hebrews 11:6)

CHAPTER 18

When I answered the call of God and said, "Yes, Lord," that was only the beginning. He gave me a vision—a goal toward which to press forward. God had left no doubt in my mind. I would be in Akron as long as I lived. I told the people the Lord was going to give us a great church. I knew, also, He would lead us, through our church services, to present the Gospel by means of television to every state in the entire Union. My decision was made. Now it was up to the Lord.

My brother-in-law, Wayne Jones, was also experiencing the admonition of God. He came to me and declared, "Rex, if you decide to stay in Akron, I'd like to stay too, if you'll have me. I'm certain the Lord wants me here."

After Wayne's return from Miami, his employer had offered him a permanent position with incredible possibilities. Wayne, however, was not to be deterred from his resolve for God. As far as financial arrangements were concerned, only the Lord knew what the future would bring. The position offered him would pay three times more than the best he could expect in the Lord's work. But tempting offers could not blot out the call of God he'd received the day he'd been saved. He put God first.

With the assistance of my good friend Clare Conlan, in

February, 1953, I took out a charter under the State of Ohio and organized Calvary Temple, Inc. A few days later when my family pulled out with the tent loaded onto the trucks, I stood there watching them go. I swallowed. Here I was with a church charter, no church members, and a little over fifty dollars in my pocket. And then I smiled, remembering it wasn't all I possessed. I had God and a vision to reach the lost with the Gospel. With that, I had everything.

As soon as possible we started looking for a home for our new church. Copley Auditorium had recently been purchased by WAKR for a television studio. We were notified they would take possession on April 1, 1953, the day our lease expired.

I had to find a place immediately. I pulled the money from my pocket, counting it carefully. $63...$64...$65—that was all there was. The realization almost swamped me. What could we possibly get with assets of only $65? I was willing to rent some building temporarily, but there was nothing available. We then looked for land on which to build. There was nothing we wanted or could afford. Next we inquired about a building to buy. We crossed the High Level Bridge, on the north side of Akron, into the city of Cuyahoga Falls. There we noticed the Ohio Theater situated prominently on State Road. It was big enough. It was in an excellent location. It had distinct possibilities. But the cost was prohibitive! They wanted $65,000 for the down payment. All I had between me and poverty at the present moment was $65.

Calling a meeting of our loyal friends in Akron, I requested the people to make pledges of what they would or could give within a three-month period. I had no idea of what building we could secure, but we needed to have some idea of how much money we could expect. Without a doubt, we had to locate a suitable spot soon. The pledges came in, and they

135

were good. It gave me heart to press on.

Meanwhile, every conference I'd had with the owners of the Ohio Theater resulted in a reduction of the price and terms. It surely looked as if God meant us to have that building. But the price they were asking and the price we could pay were still miles apart.

One day when my wife and I were walking through the place looking around, I glanced up to see Maude Aimee standing at the side with her hand on the wall. She was praying, "God, if this is the building You've picked out for us, help us to get it."

I decided to take the initiative in the transaction. After checking the pledges, I figured out the very best deal I could make. I offered the owners $5,000 at the signing of the papers, another $5,000 the day we took possession, and $5,000 a month in payments for a year. Later, we arranged to cut the monthly payments to $2,500, for we realized extensive remodeling would be necessary.

Hearing about my offer to the Ohio Theater owners, our friends scoffed and told me we hadn't a chance. They predicted the owners would never accept the offer. I just smiled. From a business standpoint it was hopeless. But I knew God was on our side.

To everyone's astonishment, the owners immediately accepted. Possession of the new Calvary Temple was arranged to take place early in March. The alterations were sketched out and we set to work, anticipating an opening date of April 5, 1953, on Easter Sunday. Maude Aimee was appointed the official decorator, and it wasn't long before she was making arrangements about everything, right down to the most minor details. I ordered a big neon cross, 42 feet high, for the exterior, so that folks would be able to see the red and green lights miles away. We wanted everyone to know this was no longer a theater, but a church dedicated to the winning of lost souls.

In the midst of all this work which threatened to consume all my time, both day and night, I faced a new task. I was now pastor of what was becoming a large congregation. It was a tough job. With all our remodeling, I continued broadcasting three times a day and preaching at the services in our old auditorium. There was little opportunity to be alone with God.

One day I had my Bible balanced on the edge of the platform, trying to snatch a moment or two for study. Two workmen had just turned away after consulting me on some figures. Then Clare Conlan strode up.

"What in the world are you doing? Back in World War II, I heard about 'Praise the Lord and Pass the Ammunition' but I've never heard of 'Read the Bible and Pass the Hammer.'" He chuckled again as he saw more workmen headed my way.

Even under the barrage of his friendly teasing it was an effort to relinquish my former thoughts and catch his mood. "Clare, I've got to get some time for study. I keep thinking of all the days ahead when these people will need to know the lessons God has promised to reveal to me as their leader."

Clare paused a second, thinking, and then suddenly his face brightened. "Rex, I have just the solution. I've a trailer down in St. Petersburg, Florida, just waiting for you! Why don't you take some time off and go down there? We can get along without you for a few days."

"That's the most generous offer you could make, Clare," I acknowledged and jabbed his shoulder affectionately. "I'm not going to be modest and refuse, because I'm depending on God to make me ready. I desperately need time alone with Him." Clare knew the thanks came from my heart.

Thinking it over later, I decided to persuade Maude Aimee that she should get away for a rest, also. But when I broached the subject, she was firm in her refusal.

"Rex, I can't take the time. This week will be too short, as it is. I've got to be here to keep the work moving. Go along by yourself, honey. We'll be all right."

She mounted a ladder and dangled some fabric from a rod. I could see her decision was final.

A week before opening day we moved out of Copley Auditorium. Maude Aimee drove me to the Cleveland Airport. The crisp March breeze was blowing as I waved goodbye. In my heart I knew she needed the trip as much as I. This bad cold she'd been fighting was serious. But ignoring the discomfort, she'd just kept going—bringing in supplies, checking deliveries, choosing colors. I dreaded to see the effects of this pressure on her by the time I returned.

The week in Florida rolled by more quickly than an Arkansas storm can rip through a country field. Once more I found myself at the airport in Cleveland, this time returning home. I was eager to see the church. Before I left town, it had taken considerable imagination to picture what the new building would look like. Scaffolds were up, tools lying around, carpeting half laid—everything in a general mess. Remembering this, once again I was struck with the size of our venture.

Maude Aimee greeted me warmly with the news that the people had worked all night the night before in order to finish last minute details, so I could see the church at 10 o'clock that morning. But no sooner. I paced up and down, feeling caged. I wanted to go right down to see the church, but Maude Aimee insisted we give our loyal friends the time they'd requested.

In those two hours at home, I grew increasingly conscious of the sacrifice my wife had made. Her cold was much worse. She seemed more tired than I could ever remember her being. I was concerned about her. . .deeply concerned. As for myself, I was feeling fine. The time I'd spent in Florida was time shared with the Lord—time for studying which had paid off in an increase of my faith. Though I'd preached a couple of times during that week—once for Clem in the "Gospel Big Top" and once when I went over to see Dr. A.E. Sprouell in Tampa, I was rested, full of ideas for the future of this ministry and full of confidence as a result of my time alone with God.

Ten o'clock finally came. We pulled up outside the church and I rushed for the entrance, anxious to look around. In the half-light of the new auditorium I paused, not able to say a word, not even able to control the tears. God had given me this wonderful church. "My cup runneth over," flashed in my mind.

Quietly I made my way to the front of the auditorium and faced the pulpit. This was the place toward which, for years, God had been directing me. He'd trained me. He'd polished the rough edges. He'd made my heart tender and fixed upon me an overwhelming burden for the lost. This pulpit was my place of service.

Right then I made some promises to God—vows I would never forget, vows that would guide me throughout my ministry. I promised I would give an altar call at every service held in Calvary Temple. I promised to pray fervently for our people, following the Lord's commands when they were sick and in trouble, counseling them when I could help ease their load. I told the Lord that when needs and financial burdens were met, I would never accumulate or hoard God's money. I vowed to reach out for new horizons, for there would always be work to be done. "Today is the day of the Lord," I repeated, and promised to listen and try to follow the guidance of the Holy Spirit, both in my personal life and in my work for the Lord. Now we had a pact—the Lord and I. He had done His part and promised He always would. I gave Him my part—the pledge for a ministry centered in Jesus

Christ, given over entirely to His glory.

I roamed over the newly decorated building. There were a few people still working, cleaning up jobs which had to be done in time for Open House that evening. They looked weary, and yet their eyes shone brightly. Just two days before, they had almost thrown up their hands in despair. Now it was touching to see their pride as all the pieces fitted together at the last minute and the church was ready, at last.

Later that day my wife and I acted as the official reception committee, greeting each person who entered the building—more than a thousand in number, before the evening was over. These were the people who had given their service to the Lord for the new church, and for this He had returned a double measure of His blessing.

Easter Sunday morning dawned grayly. What began as a patter of rain soon turned to a downpour. This was the day of our first Sunday School, and we'd been broadcasting the announcement, hoping and praying for a good crowd. We'd asked God for 1,000 in Sunday School that morning. God didn't let us down. Despite the rain, when the roll was taken, the count came to exactly 1,027.

After the service, again Maude Aimee and I greeted people at the door. Because of her exhaustion and severe respiratory infection, Maude Aimee's voice had been reduced to a croak. When the Easter worship service started, her voice was completely gone. I walked toward the platform as the service began, and tears streamed from my eyes. I could barely see where I was going and I wondered how I could conduct the service. I called Maude Aimee to come forward for her solo, but she shook her head. She couldn't even talk, much less sing. I asked the audience to join me in prayer for her, and then I placed my hand on her and prayed the Lord to heal her throat so she could sing for His glory. In an instant God answered that prayer. The piano modulated into the introduction and she stepped to the microphone. Her bell-like tone soared out over the auditorium as she sang a favorite of almost everyone there—"We'll Talk It Over."

In the afternoon another service was held. The crowd appeared to be almost as large as the one in the morning had been. Everyone felt the presence of God. After the service ended, many people sat quietly or visited in the lobby, willing to remain in order to be assured of good seats for the evening service ahead.

When seven o'clock rolled around, the auditorium, normally seating a thousand, was so packed that chairs had to be placed in every available free space, and still people were left standing.

I spoke to them simply, from a full heart. I told them how much I appreciated their efforts. Once again I repeated how thankful to God I was for all these blessings. I asked Maude Aimee to join me in our thanksgiving, but she was on the verge of tears, almost too touched to speak.

I smiled, trying to ease the strain. "Well, honey, at least tell them you're glad you married me."

She stepped to the pulpit. Her voice was choked with emotion as she testified, "Friends, I am glad I married Rex. We've had a wonderful marriage. Some of it has been hard, but we've always been happy. The Lord has been so good to us. I only hope God will continue to keep Rex as humble and thankful for God's blessings as he was this morning when he walked down the aisle with tears streaming down his face."

I put my arm around her and looked out over the congregation. Here was the work the Lord had entrusted to me. The realization was overwhelming. There was a long pause, and then I added these words, "I can only praise the Holy Name of our Lord—for bringing us here to Akron to spend the rest of our lives, laboring for Him and for His glory."

"But as we were allowed of God to be put in trust with the gospel, even so we speak; not as pleasing men, but God, which trieth our hearts."
(I Thessalonians 2:4)

CHAPTER 19

The Akron Beacon Journal ran a report of our new church's opening: "They've arrived—Rex Humbard and his family of musical evangelists. . .whose proposed advent into Cuyahoga Falls with Calvary Temple had been creating quite a stir, especially on State Road where he and his congregation purchased the old Ohio Theater to remodel it into a handsome church home. . .

"In the space of three short weeks. . .a prayer room has been made from the coal bin. . .the projection booth is now a radio broadcasting studio. . .and a photographic darkroom has replaced a tiny kitchen. . .Calvary Temple even has a special "bawl room" with cribs and baby accoutrements and a picture window overlooking the auditorium. . ."

They went on to describe the opening day's events which brought thousands into the church the first day. It seemed to stun the whole city.

So much had happened. We had incorporated the church on February 13, 1953, had elected a Board of Trustees and secured a church home. Now it was time to receive charter members. We announced the church doors would be open throughout the month of April, and those who wished to join in membership that month would be listed as charter members. All who met at the Cross of Jesus Christ as ransomed sinners, saved by His grace, were welcome to our group.

People of all denominations had been praying for a revival in the city of Akron. Now they'd seen souls saved at our every service, and they took this as an answer to their prayers. With a wide cross-section of denominations for background, the interdenominational ministry of the church was born. Christians were persuaded to lay aside doctrinal issues which so often divide the body of believers. They were reminded that by one Spirit we are baptized into the Body of Jesus Christ. God honored this emphasis. At every service sinners continued to come to repentance at our altars, through the power of God.

During the first thirty days of the initial ministry of Calvary Temple, over five hundred people became charter members. Crowds were so large that, frequently, sinners eager to find Christ would have to come back three or four times before they could get in the doors. We had no idea who had been turned away, but by God's mercy many came back, and when they did they responded to the invitation to find salvation in Christ Jesus.

Space for Sunday School became an immediate problem. We simply didn't have the facilities to handle the number which flocked to the church's educational program. It appeared the Lord was leading us to lease, for Sundays, the entire building of a large grade school twelve blocks away. There, at Grant School, the children could attend classes, leaving only the adults in the Calvary Temple building.

Transportation was the next thing to consider. Eventually, every Sunday we were to lease 22 city buses from the Akron Transportation Company in order to pick up people in the city who had no way to come to church. The buses then transported the children from Calvary Temple to their

Sunday School classes and junior church in Grant School, returning them to Calvary Temple and their waiting parents at noon. Only a short time passed before Grant School was no longer large enough for the number of boys and girls enrolled, so we leased a brand new school a bit farther away—Bolich Junior High.

Those early months brought tremendous blessing. Dr. O.E. Sprouell arrived from Tampa for our initial revival the first month. He was followed by our old friend Dr. Glenn Tingley of Birmingham, Alabama. Many lost souls found Christ in those early meetings.

We also began organizing different aspects of a well-rounded church program—music, missions, youth programs, prayer groups. Very little time had elapsed after our opening before we had an eighteen-piece orchestra and an enthusiastic choir directed by Bill Everingham, a young man devoting extraordinary time and energy to making the musical portion of the services inspiring.

The first missionary-emphasis service brought over a thousand people into the building, with hundreds turned away. The entire offering from this meeting was sent to the foreign mission field, and this began a very important part of our ministry.

For the young people we began showing Bible films on Friday nights and then added illustrated sermons acted out with costumes and scenery every Saturday night. These programs were enthusiastically attended by people of all ages, and they answered the question, "Where can a Christian go on Saturday night?" for dedicated young people throughout the city.

Under Wayne's instruction, the Adult Bible Class expanded rapidly, soon completely filling the auditorium. The church printing department turned out a monthly devotional publication, "Echoes from Calvary," and this was distributed widely in the area. A prayer room was open 24 hours a day for meditation and counseling; to this department were directed visits and telephone calls from people all over Ohio. Prayer groups were organized under the leadership of Reverend George Pryor, who also headed the visitation program. Shortly, there were more than 30 prayer groups in the city.

Programs featuring the Humbard family were being broadcast on numerous stations. We added five television stations for viewing, as well. I preached every Sunday, not missing a service at the church for the next seven and a half years.

Almost a year after Calvary Temple had opened, I was musing about the activities and I turned to Wayne and said, "The auditorium isn't large enough to hold these enormous crowds, Wayne. We're going to have our first anniversary soon. We've got to make plans to expand the seating facilities."

"How could it be done, Rex? This place has been ideal in every other way—plenty of parking. . .a central location. How can we possibly expand and retain the advantages we have?"

"I have no idea. But I've learned when a person asks the Lord to guide him right, he won't make a wrong decision about anything—where to go, what job to take, what house to buy, what to do! No matter how big or how small the situation is, if a man trusts Him, the Lord's not going to let him down."

"I believe that too, Rex. But expanding this building sure looks impossible right now."

I guess tackling problems in the previous years had made me even more determined. "We'll trust God, Wayne . . . and listen every minute before we decide—and then listen afterwards, too, for reassurance that we've heard Him right. He'll show us His instructions. God is never wrong. If we're on His side, that's all that counts."

"If any of you lack wisdom, let him ask of God, that giveth to all men liberally, and upbraideth not; and it shall be given him. But let him ask in faith, nothing wavering." (James 1:5,6)

CHAPTER 20

The first anniversary of Calvary Temple had come and gone. The ministry was growing unbelievably. We'd put in what we called a "spiritual clinic," a counseling service open from 10 a.m. until noon each day and manned by volunteers. Scores of people came daily for help. The results were tremendous.

We also had instituted a "Dial-a-Prayer" service. I changed the recorded message for it each day. In addition, we now had three radio programs every day—at 9:30 a.m.; at 10 p.m.; and from 12:30 to 1:30, shortly after midnight. Response to the services had been so vigorous that we were feeding the church service via television to six TV stations in Ohio, Pennsylvania, and West Virginia. We also televised five days a week at 6:15 p.m., Monday through Friday.

Our outreach had grown—and not just by chance. It was because we were working! And the members could clearly see that I was pushing every bit as hard as they were. We shared the burden together.

I found myself preaching five times on Sundays—at 8:30 a.m., then again at 9:30 a.m., and the third time in the morning at the 11 o'clock worship service. I delivered a message for the afternoon service which began at 3 p.m., and finally finished with a sermon for the evening service at 7 o'clock. Despite this heavy schedule, there were many I never got to talk to or even see. With city buses carrying the children to services at the public school buildings, I lacked any opportunity to contact the younger ones, as I wished to do.

Now we definitely had to make a decision. We must expand. Having consulted architects, we found we could enlarge the auditorium by "kicking out" both sides of the building and then adding an educational building across the back of the church plant. But even before the final detailed sketches were returned from the architect's office, we'd already outgrown the building as we'd planned it—the building which would still take us a year and a half to construct!

We looked around for another building to buy. Farther north on State Road was the attractive new State Theater. Television had caused its business to fall off drastically. The building seated 1,800, and we seriously considered buying it. We could enlarge the auditorium, adding an educational wing alongside. The management of the theater was considering our offer. Before we could conclude arrangements, however, we'd already passed the attendance mark we'd anticipated and outgrown our plans for the State Theater, as well.

Weeks of prayer and consultation followed. The conclusion was apparent. We would have to purchase a large block of ground and begin building a big church. With this in mind, we started to scour the local scene to see what was available.

The land at 2700 State Road, across the street from a shopping center then under construction, was occupied by a golf driving range under lease to the Kosar Golf Manufacturers, an organization producing custom golf equipment. The lease ran for another eight years. It was commonly known that this land was for sale by the owner. But it was also rumored the Kosars refused to give up their eight-year lease and thus were preventing the sale.

An opportunity arrived for me to consult the owner of the land about the possibility of our purchasing it. He stated it would cost $250,000. I knew the price was inflated and suggested an alternate figure. He remained firm. Because of the fast growth of our church and the publicity about us, it was obvious he was determined to wring a quarter of a million dollars from us for land which wasn't worth it. About that time I realized we wouldn't be able to lower the price to a reasonable level, so I gave up on the site.

But God had other plans. When I prayed, more and more I became aware of the fact the Lord wanted us to have that plot of ground. I called a real estate agent in Cuyahoga Falls, a man who was not then widely known in the business community, and told him my plan. Then I gave him our church check for $1,400 and asked him to deposit it in his account. He was to get into his car, drive to the city of Canton—twenty-five miles south, drive back to Akron and go to the First National Tower to ask to see the attorney representing negotiations on this piece of land.

He followed my instructions exactly. Returning to Akron from Canton, he went to the lawyer's office and began his explanation: "Sir, I have just come from Canton. I have a client who'd like to make an offer for the acreage at the corner of State Road and Portage Trail in Cuyahoga Falls, and I'm offering a purchase price of $140,000. Here's my check for one percent of that sum for an option to buy."

The attorney's face lighted as he eagerly accepted the check for $1,400. The property had been for sale for a long time, and he wanted to finalize the purchase as soon as possible. The option was granted, and then my real estate broker revealed his plot. His driving to Canton and then back to Akron had been a decoy, but he had told the exact truth. The real estate agent went on to explain we knew the price had been inflated. He said we were interested in the property for a reasonable price—the amount it would be quoted to others involved in a similar venture.

The attorney's face turned dull red. He'd been so sure if the Humbards and Calvary Temple bought it, he'd have been able to ram through the original figure. He knew he'd been dealing with Christians, and they were usually so eager to get what they wanted, they'd settle for anything! But now the option was on. The deal was settled.

Adjacent to the property were two other blocks of land on which were situated two farmhouses. The owners of these were interested in selling, and we were able to include these plots in our package of land.

Now the real test began—how to purchase that eight-year lease from the Kosars so we could begin to build immediately. I went to Mike and Emil Kosar and straightforwardly laid out our plans to build a church. When I finished, I asked them to figure what they felt they would make as a profit, above expenses, for the next eight years with their golfers' driving range. Time passed as they pondered carefully and arrived at an answer. I promised to pay them that exact amount.

Two days afterwards, the *Akron Beacon Journal* declared in headlines—"Calvary Temple Will Build Their New 'Cathedral of Tomorrow'," and then amplified the story, telling about the sixteen acres of land recently purchased by the church. We were on our way!

Weeks passed in a flurry of activity. We sold church bonds, raised cash and paid the price of the land. In less than 90 days, we received title to the entire sixteen acres.

Then unexpectedly, one day a man came to see me, offering the church two homes across the street from our building site, on property at the corner of Portage Trail. Along with the houses went five acres of land. The offer was tempting. But we had no money. The suggested down payment was $5,357.

A friend of mine who, strangely enough, didn't attend our church services, counseled me on the matter. "You need that land to protect your future expansion. If your church will buy the property, I'll give a gift of $5,000 for it."

The congregation was notified of the offer and they voted to pay the remaining $357. Almost in a daze at the suddenness of the transaction, Wayne and I and our respective families moved into the new church parsonages.

We now had land for future expansion, acreage totaling 21 acres in all. No man could have done all this. "God" was the answer. Our praise went to Him.

"That the trial of your faith, being much more precious than of gold that perisheth, though it be tried with fire, might be found unto praise and honour and glory at the appearing of Jesus Christ: Whom having not seen, ye love." (I Peter 1:7,8)

CHAPTER 21

We had the property, but yet, financially, we were unable to start construction immediately. Still we faced the predicament of providing space for services. On the new property I put up a tent large enough to seat several thousand. For the next two months I held evangelistic services there five nights a week, as well as continuing to conduct our regular services.

Then God nudged me. It was time to get started with our building. I went to New York, then far west to Los Angeles, south to Dallas, north to Chicago, asking for a 40% or 50% mortgage on a two and a half million dollar project. It was impossible to secure.

The contractor who had built the shopping center across the street from the church property offered to construct the church for me and also obtain the financing. Mr. E.J. DeBartolo was one of the largest contractors in the state of Ohio, but, to his surprise, he discovered he could get any amount of financing for shopping centers but none for churches. His disappointment didn't hamper my faith.

I knew the trite old saying, "Where there's a will, there's a way." Thinking it over, I added my own philosophy: "God helps those who help themselves." And then I frosted the cake of my determination with the Biblical admonition, "Faith without works is dead." I got going!

The original vision I'd had was to build a big church, and through the ministry of this, by means of coast to coast television, take the Gospel to every state in the Union. My church board was in complete agreement. But no one else wanted to assume leadership in the project.

In a church business meeting the congregation voted Rex Humbard to be head of the Architectural Committee. Then they named Rex Humbard as chairman of the Building Committee and the Finance Committee. Later they submitted the same name for spokesman of the Construction Committee. In essence, they were saying, "It's your idea. Go ahead!"

I had the total backing of the church, but no one else would step to the helm. The awesome responsibility almost swamped me. I bowed my head and prayed, "I can't do this alone. It's too big a job. But I know nothing is too big for You, Lord. So if You'll do it, I'll help."

The architectural plans had to come first. I wanted a round building topped with a dome to symbolize the world. Supporting this would be 48 pillars, representing the 48 states which were then part of the Union. I'd promised God we'd send the story of the redeeming grace of Jesus Christ in a world-wide missions program. Even the structure of the church must speak of that goal.

No architect in the cities of Akron or Cleveland would agree to design a round building such as I'd described. "It's not practical," they objected. "You can't bend pipes. You angle them. Square corners are essential."

It seemed I had come to a halt right at the very beginning. I heard of an architect in Chicago who had helped design several unusual buildings. I flew to Chicago, and that afternoon again I described my concept of our new Cathedral to A.L. Salzman and his three sons, the latter recently having been graduated from the Architectural Division of the University of Illinois. The words that I used seemed to take wings. I told them how the main auditorium must seat over 5,000 people. I needed two things—plans for the building and sufficient financing. My dream was in their hands.

The father, A.L. Salzman, followed my every syllable. He was so impressed with what the Lord had led me to say he frightened his three sons by declaring stoutly, "He's going to build this church, and we're going to help him!"

"Thank you for your confidence, Mr. Salzman. And what about your terms?" I inquired softly.

"Here's our deal, Reverend Humbard. We will be paid the standard architectural fees. We'll design the building and help supervise the construction of it. Then we'll ask for our money when you are finally in your building, have secured the mortgage and have the money to pay us. Not before."

They kept their word. They were not paid until five years after the Cathedral of Tomorrow was officially opened. They never asked for their money in all those years and kept their part of the deal to the letter. Those men had my unbounded respect and admiration. I knew God had chosen them to help me. I pray He will bless them in the future for their sacrifice and goodwill.

It wasn't long before I had a broomstick, plus a set of slides and a projector to show the congregation what the building would look like. Those sketches were exactly like the church as it stands today. After viewing them, the faces in the audience lighted up. Our prayers took on new meaning. Sight had stimulated faith.

Though I was still unable to secure full financing, through banking circles I was promised a one-third mortgage on a turn-key job. That is to say, I would pay when the building was open and in use. This was the best financing I was able to locate. I'd tried everything I knew.

I formulated a plan in my mind and asked the contractor to carry this one-third until I was in the church, had sold church bonds and raised the money in the building fund for the other two-thirds. I now had the plans. I had the land. But there was no money on hand.

I flew back to Chicago for another conference with the Salzmans.

"Could you start the job if I gave you $25,000 this week?"

Mr. Salzman's smile was sympathetic but amused. "Reverend Humbard, let me fill you in on the picture. The diameter of the circle of the church is 300 feet. That means the circumference of the outer wall will be 943 feet around. The concrete footers will be five feet wide, and these must be reinforced with steel. For that money, the men couldn't even dig the holes, let alone pour the concrete and set in the steel."

I lifted my chin and stared him straight in the eye. "Well, couldn't you just dig a little. . .and pour a little. . .and put in a little steel? By the time you've finished with that, I'm sure we'll have some more money. You see, Mr. Salzman, we've got to have action if we're going to build this church. We have to take it out of the talking stage."

That was Thursday afternoon. By Monday morning I'd borrowed the $25,000 from a friend and had deposited it in a bank for a construction account. The Salzman Company had arrived to drive in a stake in the very center of the circle. A gigantic bulldozer and a steam shovel were digging that tiny, little hole!

The *Beacon Journal* blazoned the headline "Construction Started!" And our own church members chanted joyously, "We've started building our church!" And God's people were coming across those grounds looking for God's servant to help make that tiny, little hole into a bigger hole!

I let all the contracts for the construction. Maude Aimee became the interior decorator. Together we supervised the entire project. In her high heels she'd climb ladders, talk to contractors and check to see the work was being done efficiently and on time. The workmen would do things for her they'd never do for me.

"How about staying with it for another hour?" she'd suggest, after crawling up to the dome. And they'd grin as they started in again, weariness forgotten.

For two years I originated my three daily programs from that site, while the Cathedral was being built. In the winter I stood in the cold, with boots and gloves, hat and coat. In summer I stood in the sun and told the people about the building progress. It was a structure dedicated to the interest of humanity and the opportunity God had promised us to win souls for Him.

Jewish men, Catholics, Protestants, non-Christians—all held contracts and helped me coordinate the work. For when a man lets a contract without money, it has to be reinforced with men who believe in him and in what he represents. We kept our part of the bargain. The contractors carried the one-third amount which the bank had promised to pay when the Cathedral was opened to the public.

Those months were hard months. Construction always is. But they were months characterized by faith. They were months when the Lord demonstrated His power. We saw daily miracles—big ones and small ones. There were people who found Christ right in the midst of plaster dust and lumber shavings. It was sacred ground.

God had tried us in His fire. He refined us as gold. Only the vision of what He had promised kept us driving forward.

In our hearts we heard the Word of God as it would be exalted from the pulpit of this structure. We pictured the results as the Gospel would be sent out to hungry hearts

throughout the world. The worth of a soul—that was what
made every moment of that struggle a triumph!

"Being confident of this very thing, that He which hath begun a good work in you will perform it until the day of Jesus Christ."(Philippians 1:6)

CHAPTER 22

Saturday, May 24, 1958. That was the day. Sixty thousand people would celebrate the opening of the Cathedral of Tomorrow, before that day was over.

In the morning ten thousand gathered to view the March of Youth Parade, which began at Calvary Temple and traversed the two miles up State Road to the new church. An airplane flew lazy figure eights overhead and then headed south toward Akron, trailing the banner: "Tonight—The Cathedral of Tomorrow." On every light post in Cuyahoga Falls and on down Akron's Main Street were shields bearing crossed flags, usually used for the Soap Box Derby, but now announcing, "Welcome—Opening, Cathedral of Tomorrow."

The Radio Bible Club Assembly, 600 in number, led the grand march. Then followed the floats carrying the Youth Band and floral designs of a huge Bible, proudly proclaiming, "On the Move for Christ." Drum majors heightened the excitement. In small-boy embarrassment, the Sunday School Boys' Baseball Team moved forward. They were proud of their costumes and prouder still, as they walked those city blocks, to testify of their love for the One they served.

When the marchers-for-Christ reached the Cathedral, they filled the cross-shaped concourse in front of the building.

They knelt in prayer, and David Gibbs, Christian education director, asked the Lord's blessing upon the building and its world-wide ministry. In the bright May sunshine, both the Christian flag and the American flag billowed in the breeze. It was a moment of great thanksgiving.

I stepped forward to join in the dedication. "This building is a miracle—a miracle that could only happen in America, land of the free. And to God we give the glory."

In the afternoon I directed a tour televised by WAKR-TV and WJW-TV and fed to stations throughout Ohio, Pennsylvania and West Virginia. Assembled were all the contractors and suppliers who had had a hand in the building. I reviewed the construction wonders, mentioning the details which had led Paul Metzler, art editor of the *Cleveland Plain Dealer,* to announce: "It is the wood engineering marvel of the century." He had gone on to describe it more fully. "It is the world's largest domed gathering place for religion, with a wood-domed canopy four inches thick and a vaulting span of 220 feet. In contrast to this, the second in size, the Cathedral of Florence in Italy, has a dome diameter of only 138 and a half feet."

Everyone seemed to catch his breath as we moved past the black-veined ebony granite entrance, crossed the lobby and entered the main auditorium. No interior supports marred the expanse of the 38,000 square foot black dome. I heard murmured comments about the tear drop chandeliers and the huge cross, measuring 100 feet in length, said to be the largest indoor cross in the world. I pointed out that the cross was designed to reflect the moods of the programs. Right then, technicians demonstrated some of the more than 60 different color combinations possible.

I explained there was permanent seating for 5,400. Then we moved down the aisles toward the front of the auditorium. The 168-foot stage, brightened by a red crushed velvet contour curtain, drew the crowd's attention. But I was looking at the pulpit. While the visitors exclaimed about all the hydraulic lifts and remote controls, I was thinking that the real focus was that pulpit. . .and what it meant.

There were so many other things to see—the 200-bed nurseries, the chapels, the prayer room for counseling, the library, 154 classrooms—all this, and more. On the tour I introduced my brother-in-law, Wayne Jones, as associate pastor. Then I went on to present the rest of the ministerial staff: George Pryor; Dave and Pearl Gibbs, the children's workers; and Jackie Burris, who had joined our staff to supervise the missions program. He had been an evangelist in 72 countries and shared my burden for the millions abroad without Christ. Finally I introduced Will Chandler, the young people's director who himself would soon feel the call of missions and go to serve in Dakar, West Africa.

Maude Aimee had helped to program the tour, organizing it so we'd be ready for the final interview. First to speak was A. E. Salzman. He and his sons had brought their families, and with great pride they showed the building and spoke of their friendship.

A chuckle arose from the crowd when Mr. Salzman finished his speech and his young grandson spoke up. "Grandpa, who's the rabbi here?"

"Why, Rex is," Mr. Salzman replied and fondly patted the youngster's head.

From that moment on, the lad's big brown eyes regarded me with awe.

There were many others who spoke that day. As they did, I kept wanting them all to see it as I saw it, not just as a magnificent building, but as a fountainhead for world evangelism. I told them this as the tour closed.

"The Cathedral of Tomorrow was built by man, but it was created by God. I am not impressed with its grandeur. It isn't the building that's important. It's what's going on in it that's important—a world-wide program for God."

That day passed so quickly. I spent hours shaking hands with my dear friends. There were civic officials to greet, governmental visitors like Fred Danner from the State Senate and Bill Ayers from the United States House of Representatives, both of whom had come to wish us well and encourage us for the work ahead. My parents were there from Hot Springs to join in the celebration, and Wayne's mother had arrived from Detroit.

The official opening that night would exceed our greatest hopes. From West Virginia, Pennsylvania, New York and all parts of Ohio the people came. They arrived in cars, in buses, some even in trucks. Over 7,500 streamed inside, filling the building. They were crowded into nurseries, lined up in the halls. Thousands were turned away. For the next twelve nights I was to stand behind that pulpit to preach the Gospel of Jesus Christ, to see those altars filled with hundreds wanting to give their lives to Christ. And this was opening night.

I had prepared a simple salvation message, the story from the Gospels of the Cleansing of the Leper. I wanted those people to believe what that leper believed when he looked to the Saviour and cried, "Lord, if Thou wilt, Thou canst make me clean." By God's grace, this night they could find their sins forgiven, cleansed for eternity.

This was what God had called me to do—to bring lost souls to Him. This was the reason He'd led me all those years in ways I could not fathom. This was the purpose of the magnificent building God had provided. Here was the answer to my prayer.

As the service began, the fanfare sounded and the crowd

grew silent. The kleig lights brightened. The cameras began to roll. The heat of the lights touched the pulpit, and I stepped forward.

For a moment I felt speechless. Tears filled my eyes. And then I said, "Today . . . we've put God on Main Street."

This was the Lord's doing, and it is marvelous in our eyes? (Mark 12:11)

Joyce Parks grew up in Cuyahoga Falls, Ohio, not far from the present site of the Cathedral of Tomorrow. Having graduate degrees in the field of speech, Miss Parks has served as a professor in the Department of Public Speaking of Bob Jones University, Greenville, South Carolina. For several years she has been associated with Rex Humbard's work and admires his simple faith and his deep concern for the lost.